CW01637936

STAND BACK TO GROW

Make Your Business Work Without You

Michael K Krajewski and Jeff Cox*

* Co-author of *The Goal*

Stand Back to Grow

Authors' Note

Michael was born in South Africa of Polish parents and has lived in England since 2007. Jeff is American. So this is a genuine transatlantic collaboration. Unfortunately Webster's and the Oxford English dictionaries don't collaborate so well with spelling. So we struggled with whether to use British or US spelling. In the end we decided on US, but it could just as easily have been British.

Introduction

The idea of starting a business is a dream for many. Having a business of one's own seems like the perfect path to freedom, allowing the would-be entrepreneur to escape the restrictions and demands of jobs that typically consume most of the waking hours of the employed. Becoming your own boss – what a wonderful notion that is.

I should know. Some years ago, I was drawn in by the dream. I was working for an engineering company and I was doing very well. The money I was making was good. My work was viewed as being top-notch. Yet I wanted something more. So I began contemplating a jump to entrepreneurship – and it was very exciting.

What happened to me happens to a lot of people. In the months leading to the business start-up, we tend to see the world as if through rose-colored glasses. We're embarking on a great adventure! What could go wrong? The possibility of failure is ignored. Instead, there is an infatuation with success. And there is the allure of earning a lot of money, far more than one could earn as an employee. Once the decision to open your own business takes hold, entrepreneurship can become an obsession.

A major problem, however, is that very few of those starting a business have the right kind of knowledge or experience necessary to make it succeed. The education system teaches us to become employees, not business owners, and business schools teach students to become high-level managers for corporations. Those who want to become business owners face a yawning gap in terms of learning how to run their companies well. Many making the switch from employee to owner don't even realize that totally different sets of skills and knowledge are required. And when they do start their businesses, they are blindsided by realities they never expected. Instead of learning in advance what to do, they are taught by the school of life, which in my view is actually a very effective teacher if the entrepreneurial student can learn quickly before disaster strikes.

Unfortunately, what tends to happen among new owners is that once sales begin to tick upward, they become slaves of their own businesses. Work becomes their life and life turns into continuous work. The anticipated freedom from the demands of corporate life never materializes and in fact is replaced by demands of the business that are far greater than what the employee has to deal with. "Freedom" becomes a mirage and no matter how hard you try, that part of the dream keeps moving further away.

A grim reality sets in. There are always problems to solve. The challenges become recurring. The quest for what the dream promised becomes a never-ending story. The working hours get ridiculously long. Family and social life take a blow. Then, often due to stress, health issues start creeping in. You end up in a self-constructed jail with no way out.

In terms of finances, quite often the salary collected by the owner is lower than was for the job he or she had before starting the business. This is like pouring salt on a sore wound and the resentment only aggravates an already bad situation. But the worst outcome is the sense of being overwhelmed as you reach your physical and mental limits.

I went through all of this. In the early years of my company, I went from feeling glee that my self-owned business was now open to being over-worked, miserable, exhausted, and depressed.

When my business made it through the first year, the money I earned was actually higher than I expected. But this taught me a lesson: money indeed does not make you happy. Although I never had suicidal thoughts, I desperately wished for a way out of my situation. I knew the world had much more to offer than what I was experiencing. I wanted to be healthy, fit and happy again. Instead, the opposite had occurred. My business had totally consumed me to the point that I was almost literally a ghost of myself.

The thought that kept me going and actually forced me to find a way out was that there were and are many business owners running multiple businesses. They employed sometimes thousands of employees. Yet these owners who had somehow gotten it right also had only 24 hours in a day, just like me. I therefore knew that what I wanted could be done, if I could just figure out *how*.

My biggest inspiration was Richard Branson – not the man himself, but his Virgin Atlantic airline with its planes flying overhead when landing at or taking off from Heathrow in London. Branson wasn't piloting the planes himself, making the meals and so on – he employed thousands of people. Yet here was I, working crazy hours with just two employees. The desire to find out about the mistakes I'd made and learn how to change things that had become dysfunctional set me on an exhilarating journey with many difficult moments and decisions on the way. This book is a fictional overview of what I experienced on that journey – a journey that, by the way, continues though I have learned so much along the way.

My mother is an academic teacher, as was my grandfather. So if there are "teaching genes" I suppose I must have some in me. My passion is to help other business owners escape from the same trap that I fell into. My way back from the brink came by way of a process that I call *Stand Back*. My ultimate goal is to help business owners regain their well-deserved balance of work and life. I want them to start enjoying life again.

My initial intention was to write the book myself. I even spent a day with a book-writing advisor who helped me prepare all the chapters, sections, etc. But when I got down to actually writing the book, I quickly realized that it would have ended up being yet another boring how-to book that people would ditch after a few chapters. It was not that the content wouldn't have been of use; the problem was the way the content was presented.

At about the same time I became a fan of Eliyahu Goldratt's books written as business novels. After some research I realized that it wasn't Dr. Goldratt who wrote the novels, but the professional writers he engaged. One day I stood in front of my bookcase and stared at one of the best business books of all time: *The Goal*. The creative writer who penned that story was an American named Jeff Cox.

Then, in that moment, a thought crept in: what if I reach out to Jeff? I immediately played down that possibility on the basis of having doubts whether it would work. On the other hand, I thought, *if I don't try I won't find out*. So I sent Jeff an email explaining the concept for the book. A few days later I received a response, eagerly awaited on my part. In short, Jeff said that he was semi-retired, but for the right project he would be willing to come out of retirement and that my concept was a good contender. Well, long story short, a few weeks later I was planning to be in California for some business training. On the way back to London, I made a stop to meet up with Jeff at his home. We spent a day together discussing the Stand Back to Grow topic, got to know each other and, that same day, signed an agreement to write this book. Working with Jeff has been a joy and each time I received more chapters to review, I couldn't believe what a genius he is! It was literally a jaw-dropping experience and I hope you feel the same when reading this book.

Entrepreneurs are wonderful people and I truly enjoy working and spending time with them. They sometimes turn out to be people who actually do change the world. When successful, they can become an inspiration for millions of others. But there are genuine difficulties to be faced. Statistics say that 90% of new businesses fail in the first 10 years. So many never rise to their potential. I want to help business owners succeed, but I also want them – you – to gain a much healthier life and self-perception.

The fact that I decided to write this business book does not mean I know everything about business – far from it. I experience the same issues that other business owners experience, but this is partly why I simply enjoy growing businesses. It is never boring. It is an exciting venture and I keep learning every day. I do however know that most business owners end up in the same trap I was once in, and because I have found a way out of it, I really wanted to reveal the solutions for others. I continue to develop my business skills and knowledge as I continue to grow my businesses and start new ventures. This book shines light on the problem and explains the things that need to change or be adopted in order to Stand Back.

I hope you enjoy the book. All credit for the creative story goes to Jeff. My goal will be achieved when this book inspires you to regain a healthy work/life balance, as at the end of the day, we only live once and we have to ensure we live our life to the fullest.

Michael K Krajewski
London, 2024

Chapter 1

Who Has The Time To Buy Rope?

Bob Bingham glanced at his calendar and saw that the appointed day of his own funeral would occur in less than 72 hours, but realized he had not as yet bought the rope with which he intended to hang himself.

"Oh nuts," he said.

He jumped up from behind his desk and went to his office window. Parting the blinds, he peered outside. The sky was dark. The hour was late. And he had no rope.

He had already paid for his funeral in advance and made all the arrangements. So, in Bob's mind, there was no turning back. He had to go through with it. In any case, he reasoned, he was gone already. His business was killing him. Yes, he was still breathing, but he had no life – except for the business, which *was* his life. And he hated it.

Indeed, he had chosen the date of his funeral because it coincided with the fifth anniversary of the day he had opened the business. What a joyful day that had been. Not anymore. The joy was long gone.

"And the name of the deceased?" the undertaker had asked Bob.

"A relative," Bob said.

"Could you be more specific, please?"

"You'll be advised of the identity at the appropriate time," Bob told him. "Until then ... "

He opened his wallet, took out a sizeable quantity of cash, and handed it to the undertaker.

"A little extra," Bob said. "For your confidentiality and discretion."

"Oh ... Well, I suppose I can be flexible. Thank you!" the undertaker said. "You know, with people living longer these days, I'm just not getting the volume that would allow me to live more comfortably."

So everything was in order – except that Bob had forgotten to buy the rope. Actually, no; he had not forgotten, he simply had not gotten around to it. Each and every day, there were one-hundred-and-one decisions that had to be made. And being the owner of this business, Bob felt compelled to make most of them himself. It was *his* business after all. Aside from the decision-making, there was the doing. The problem solving. The constant interruptions by people asking Bob what to do. His phone calls to customers to smooth things over. The chaos of things going wrong. The ongoing adjustments to make things work out. The fixing when something broke, and Bob was always the one who could make something work when all others had failed. And the delays. The expediting. The overall craziness. And today – now *tonight* – had been typical.

"All right, all right," he said to no one. "I'll go and buy the damn rope."

He said this to no one because no one else was in the building. All his employees had left and gone home hours ago. This was a normal occurrence at Bob's business. He himself would come in early, well in advance of regular business hours – arriving at 6:00 a.m. or perhaps 7:00 a.m. on a weekend – while the employees would come to work at 8:00. Then they would wrap things up around 5:00 p.m. and leave, while Bob would continue working well into the evening, departing around 10:00 p.m. or sometimes 11:00.

So he tidied up his desk and put on his jacket, which just barely fit him. Bob, who was around 40 years of age, had once been athletic, even something of a health nut. Over the past few years, however, he had been gaining weight and had become rather stout, if not fat. Working such long hours as he did, Bob was unable to get much exercise and was constantly eating ...well, every morsel he could get his fingers on, because eating was comforting, but most of those morsels came from high-calorie, high-fat, take-out food. Hence, the snugness with which his jacket fit.

From his office, Bob walked out through Assembly. What were being assembled in this area during daylight hours were Burbells, that amazing new technology that just might revolutionize the world, if it ever caught on.

Just beyond Assembly was Service. Bob had always been proud that the company not only produced Burbells, it serviced them as well. Repairs and maintenance, unique configurations, and special designs for special customers – all were available through Service. And Bob himself did most of the service work.

Then came Shipping. Bob looked with no small measure of gratification at the stacks of Burbells in a variety of vibrant colors waiting to go out, bound for applications far and wide.

He came to the building's entrance, stepped outside, locked the door behind him, and went in search of rope.

Fortunately – or unfortunately, depending upon one's viewpoint – just down the street was one of those behemoth stores that sells everything. And it was still open. Bob went inside and eventually found the aisle with rope.

So many kinds. There was nylon rope. (Too inflexible.) Clothesline. (Questionable strength; could break and drop you crashing down onto the floor.) Baling wire. (Bob shuddered at the thought of that around his neck.) Bungee cords. (No, no, no, bad idea.) And then good old traditional Manila rope. (Some might say the Rolls Royce of ropes.)

Bob selected the Manila, paid the cashier, and walked back to his office carrying the spool under his arm.

He paused briefly before unlocking the door and, believing this would be the last time he would see it, looked up at the name of his company overhead:

BURBELLS UNIVERSAL

Robert Bingham, Founder

The sign, once pristine, now seemed a bit neglected and the letters had a faded and grimy look. Bob sighed.

He went inside and through the building, footsteps on the concrete echoing, back to his office. There, he had to contend with grim practicalities. Finding a proper suspension point. Making a noose. Bob referred to the Internet. Finally he had the noose expertly tied. It dangled from the ceiling just in front of his desk. He sat down and stared at it.

For the first time, Bob was seeing the reality of what he was doing. He was now daunted by what he intended to do. Yet he could envision no other solution to his difficulties.

With hesitation and reluctance, he climbed on top of his desk. He took hold of the noose and slowly leaned forward. He was about to put his head through it – when he remembered: the suicide note.

"Dammit!"

He had forgotten to put the note out on the desk in plain sight. Now he had to climb down from the desk, log onto the company system, and look for the note he had crafted weeks before. But he couldn't find it. It was not in "Documents", not in the "cloud", not anywhere that Bob could find. What had happened to it? Then he remembered. He opened the folder of deleted files. And there it was.

He brought up the file, started reading, and then felt immediately that it was absolutely necessary to make some changes. An hour later, Bob was still editing his suicide note.

At some point, he paused. He looked at the Manila-rope noose dangling in the air above him.

"What the hell am I doing?" he asked – again, to nobody but himself.

At that moment, he became acutely aware that he was very tired. He was physically tired because of the length of the day, which as usual had been so long. Months, years of long days. And he was also so tired – so very, *very* tired – mentally and emotionally. Indeed, beyond tired. Exhausted in every way.

He felt himself nodding, drifting off. He startled himself awake a couple of times. Then he placed his head on the blotter of his desk. And he was out, asleep almost instantly.

Bob slept deeply and snored loudly. He slept all night, until well past dawn.

*

Lena Novak arrived at Burbells Universal a bit early, about 7:45. As usual, she had in hand a cardboard carrying tray with two paper cups, tea for herself and coffee for Bob. She set the tea on her work table in Assembly and headed for Bob's office with the coffee. She was a slender, blond, rather tall woman in her mid-thirties, married with two children. As she approached the door to his office, she could hear Bob snoring.

Oh no, she thought. *He slept here overnight again.*

She knocked, opened the door – and saw the noose. Lena let out a piercing, shrill scream. Bob instantly awakened. He sat bolt upright.

"Lena, what's wrong?"

"*That!* What is *that*?" she asked, pointing at the noose.

"What's it look like?"

"Bob, were you going to ... ?"

"Yes. But I didn't."

"Why?"

"Why didn't I kill myself?"

"No, of course not! Why would you want to?"

"Well, I wouldn't say I *wanted* to kill myself," Bob told her. "It's just that ... I needed a way out."

"A way out of *what?*"

"Out of *this,"* he said, making a sweeping gesture toward seemingly everything. "Out of this business! Out of my miserable life! Out of failure!"

"Failure? But I thought we were doing all right, the company that is."

"We're covering costs, Lena, but that's about all. We're not growing. And, between you and me, it looks as if we never will."

Lena was the only employee Bob trusted to any degree. Her formal title was "operations manager", but essentially she was Bob's assistant. Lena didn't really manage anything; Bob, however, managed everything. Lena simply accepted this as reality and did the best she could. Privately, she admired Bob for his many good qualities. Among others, he was visionary, technically brilliant, and fair-minded. But she had also observed that Bob meddled more than he actually managed.

"And we have to grow," Bob was telling her. "We do not have a monopoly on Burbell technology. Not at all. This company will be left in the dust of others if we can't find ways to expand."

"Well then, what's the solution?" Lena asked.

"Damned if I know!" he said. "I can't work more hours than I already do. And I can't afford to pay overtime or bring in more employees. So ultimately, it falls on me to get things done. And if something gets screwed up – as it often does if I'm not involved – we fall that much further behind."

"Bob, there must be a way ... right?"

"I hope so," he said. "But I don't know what it is. What else can I do?"

"What about a bank loan?" Lena suggested. "You know, money to allow the company to finance an expansion?"

"No, I've got enough troubles with cash flow just servicing the debt we've already got – especially given that HTI, our biggest customer, has apparently decided not to pay us!"

"What about an investor?"

"Already got one too many," Bob said.

"Who?"

"Moe."

"Moe?"

"Maurice Strickett."

"Oh, right, right. Your silent partner."

"Yes, but he's not so silent these days. He wants dividends. He's like a dog nipping at my heels – or higher on the anatomy. Legally, there is nothing he can do, but he certainly can and does make my life even more miserable than it otherwise is."

Noises came from outside Bob's office, from elsewhere in the building. The other employees were arriving for work.

"Well, I guess we should get going. Thanks for listening," Bob told her.

"Here is your coffee," she said, handing it to him. "Now, Bob, are you going to be all right?"

"I think so. No worse than any other day."

"I mean, should you see someone? A psychologist?"

"Oh, no, no, no. I don't have time for that."

"Bob, I don't mean to overstep," she said, "but maybe you should make time."

"I'll think about it."

"Please do think about it," Lena said, then added in almost a whisper, "And take down the rope."

Just as she turned to leave, there was a knock on the office door. One of the workers, Kevin Cirrus, a short but athletic twenty-ish young man, was standing in the doorframe.

"Excuse me, Mr. Bingham," Kevin said, "but we need more thera-mods. We're out."

"Completely out?" Bob asked.

"Yes, I just checked."

"Why didn't you – or somebody – tell me about this sooner?"

Kevin shrugged and said, "I don't know."

"All right, I'll get on the phone and see if I can track some down."

Then Kevin noticed the noose.

"Um, excuse me, but what is *that* doing there, Mr. Bingham? What's it for?"

"Motivation!" said Bob. "Motivation to pick up the pace around here! Unless you'd like to try it out?"

A horrified expression came over Kevin's face.

"Just kidding!" Bob assured him.

Kevin forced a grin as if he understood the joke, while Lena eased him out the door.

"So," Bob said as he untied the rope, "back to normal."

Chapter 2

Overload

Briefly, having commuted his own sentence, Bob felt glad to be alive. However, that soon passed.

Bob got on the phone to his primary thera-mod vendor. They would be happy to fill the order, but they required a two-week lead time. Obviously, that was unacceptable. So he called his secondary vendor. Yes, they had thera-mods! Yes, they were available *now!* But the price was ridiculously higher than Bob was accustomed to paying. Nevertheless, Bob placed the order. Without the thera-mods, everything would screech to a halt.

He dispatched Kevin to pick them up and turned his attention to the next crisis – and just as he was alleviating it, about an hour later, Lena came in to inform him that she had discovered they had plenty of thera-mods – boxes of them – but they had been put in the wrong place on the inventory shelves. Mere seconds later, Kevin walked in with the ridiculously expensive ones.

Bob immediately called the secondary vendor to see if the thera-mods Kevin had just picked up could be returned. Well, of course they could be returned, but there would be a 20-percent restocking fee deducted from the refund. This sent Bob's mood into full howl. Fully internally contained, of course.

And then Ned Meyers called. Ned was a prominent customer. He had requested a specially designed Burbell and Bob was personally handling that project.

After pleasantries, Ned came to the point and asked, "So how is the new design coming along?"

"It's coming along fine," Bob fibbed. "We've had a few challenges to overcome, but we're moving along."

"Good. When can I see something?"

"Soon."

"Good! How soon?"

"Well ... Um ... How about next week?"

"Next week? Fine. Wednesday?"

"Um ... No, sorry, I have a conflict on Wednesday. How about Friday?"

"I'm out on Friday," said Ned.

"Thursday? One o'clock?" Bob offered.

"Good enough. See you then."

Upon ending the call, Bob charged out of his office and over to Service. He had started to work on the design weeks before, but had been distracted by dozens of other matters. Progress on the design for Ned had stalled. Bob now pulled it up and tried to remember where he left off.

Working next to him was Gerald Lewis, better known to the other employees as "Grumpy". He was a large man who always looked a bit unkempt. Service was his domain; he was excellent at repairs and reconfigurations. But he was also a constant complainer, always muttering to himself and to others about the wrongness of the general world, lacing his comments abundantly with obscenities. However, he knew better than to complain when Bob was within earshot, so the two worked side by side in silence.

Then Lena appeared.

"Bob, the accountant just called. She needs the numbers for last month by the end of today so that she can do the tax filing."

"Arrgh!" Bob exclaimed.

He charged back to his office where he plunged into revenue and expenses, assets and liabilities and owner's equity. As he labored to bring the records up to date, lunch time came and he worked straight through it, then realized he was famished. He had Lena order fried chicken with a side dish of macaroni and cheese. He was nibbling on these while he finalized the ledger when a customer called to make a number of complex changes to his order.

And so it went until the end of the day. The employees finished their work and left the building to go back to their personal lives. Just before leaving, Lena came into Bob's office.

"I'm going home," she told him. "You should too."

"I've just got a few things to finish up."

"Finish them tomorrow. *Please.* Just go home, Bob."

He drew in a deep breath and let it out.

"All right, Lena. Thank you."

Nevertheless, Bob worked another hour in his office before leaving for home – toting along reading materials he planned to get to after dinner.

*

Bob headed home with an emotional mixture of desire and dread. When he arrived, as soon as he walked in, he felt an arctic chill. Emily, his wife, was standing at the bottom of the steps leading upstairs to the bedrooms. Her arms were crossed and she was leveling her gaze at him, her ice-blue eyes shooting a laser-straight freeze ray at him.

"Hi," said Bob.

"Who are you?" she asked. "Oh! That's right! You're my husband. How nice of you to drop by."

"Where are the kids?"

"Out. With friends. Having fun. Doing what kids do. Not that you would know what kids do."

"That's unfair," Bob told her.

"Maybe. Where were you last night?"

"At work. Where else would I be?"

"Not here. Definitely not here. Like all the other times."

"I was working. What, do you think I was having an affair?"

"I don't know what to think," said Emily. "And I'm not sure anymore that I care. I just know you weren't here."

"Would you like to know what I was really doing last night? I was getting ready to kill myself."

Emily's freeze ray powered down a bit.

"Seriously?" she asked.

"Yes."

"Why?"

"Because, among other things, I can't be with you and the kids! I mean it!"

"Well, why can't you?"

"If I'm not at work, the business will fail, that's why. We're barely squeaking through. I mean that, Emily."

"Yes, I know, you've said that before."

"I have put all the money we have into that business. If the company goes under, I'll have lost it all. That's why I work day and night so that the business will not fail, even though I believe that eventually it *will* fail."

"If it's destined to fail, why not go out of business now and spare yourself and everyone else the agony?"

"I never said it was *destined* to fail. I said, or I meant to say, that it would *probably* fail sooner or later."

"Whatever. Bob, I've been listening to you for years – on those rare occasions when we're together. To my ears, it's sounded like you've been doing the same things over and over. You're working very hard, but you're not getting anywhere. If you keep doing the same things the same way over and over, you're going to get the same crappy results. You have to change!"

"Yes, I know!" he said. "But change to what? That's the part I can't figure out."

"Well, you'd better try *something* different."

Bob sighed.

"Emily, let me just ask: Do you want a divorce?"

"No, I don't want a divorce. I want the man I married ten years ago. And you're no longer him."

He winced at the venom in her voice. She saw this and relented.

"I'm sorry, Bob. Shouldn't have said that. You know, I still do love you, but I'm so tired of being a single parent, and so angry at being neglected and taken for granted."

"I understand, Emily. I really do. I am unhappy as well. Listen, I need to lie down for a while. I'm totally beat. But when the kids get home, I'll take all of us out to dinner."

"That's a nice gesture," Emily allowed, "but it's going to take a lot more than that."

Bob stepped past her, began the climb toward their bedroom, then paused.

"Would you join me?" he asked.

"Not in the mood."

He continued up the stairs.

"Sweet dreams," she said.

*

In the morning, Bob arrived at his usual early hour. He immediately plunged into unfinished tasks and the endless minutiae of running the business. But after an hour or so, he paused and looked out the window. He felt he was on some invisible treadmill that had no "stop" button. How could he make it stop? How could he get off the treadmill? How could he manage the business and yet get a life he enjoyed?

He tried to think about what should be changed. What would make a difference? More importantly, what would make a difference in a big way? Nothing came to mind.

He did however think of a few things – little things. Like a more efficient arrangement of inventory shelving to avoid another thera-mod debacle. Yes, and better labeling to reduce mistakes and miscommunication.

But everything he thought of was in the category of little stuff – things that were incremental improvements. These were worth doing, perhaps, but none of them would make a huge difference. Their impact would be nothing that could change the game in the company's favor, nothing with enough momentum to save the business or Bob himself. Yet he did have one thought of something that might work: the employees. Why not ask them what they thought of how the business was running? Why not ask them for good old-fashioned suggestions? Nothing fancy; just find out what they thought – if indeed they did think.

Bob did not hold much hope that anything tremendously valuable would come out of an employee meeting. But he figured why not give it a shot?

*

Lena arrived, bringing her morning tea and Bob's coffee. He went out to get his cup and to reimburse Lena. He always insisted on paying for both their beverages, since she went to the trouble of picking them up.

"How are you feeling today?" she asked. "Any better?"

"A little, yes. Lena, after everyone has arrived, before we really get down to the day's work, I'd like to bring everyone together for a meeting – a brief meeting, a stand-up meeting – just to ask their opinions."

"Why, that sounds good, Bob. Seriously, that sounds like a good idea, because we don't communicate as well as we should, in my opinion."

So indeed, as soon as all had arrived, Lena called them to Assembly, the largest area of the building, and had them form a circle. Bob came in and stepped into the center of the circle to address them. He immediately felt a twinge of discomfort with all those faces staring at him, but he stiffened his resolve and tried not to let his feelings show.

"I've called all of us together," said Bob, "for a brief meeting to discuss ways we might improve company performance. After all, every one of us likes success and promotions and all of that. So here is your chance to contribute to our future. Does anyone have any suggestions on how to make the company run better?"

"I'll tell you one thing," said John, who was a large barrel-chested man, "the policy on allowing returns is way too liberal. People are returning things just because they feel like it! I say, if they bought it, they damn well ought to keep it! And if there's a problem, it's their problem, not ours! Do you know how much time I have to put into doing the paperwork? It's such a waste! So I say, no more returns!"

Bob felt his pulse rising as he searched his mind for a response.

"Thank you, John. However, I think that disallowing returns is just a little at odds with today's business climate."

"It's the wave of the future," said John, "I'm telling you."

"Right. Anyone else?" Bob asked.

Alice, a shy young woman who mainly did clerical work, tentatively raised her hand.

"Yes, Alice?"

"I think that if we celebrated each other's birthdays it would have a positive effect on morale," she said.

"Yes. Good idea," said Bob. "We'll keep that in mind. Who's next?"

Felix, a man with longish kinky red hair, spoke up.

"The DynaMicro always needs to be recalibrated and it really slows us down."

"I'm aware of that," said Bob, "but I don't think there is much to be done about it."

Then Lena spoke up.

"Bob, I say this with no disrespect to you, but ... "

"Yes? What?"

"It's just that ... well ... if we could make our own decisions and do our jobs as we see fit, things might go a lot more smoothly than they generally do."

"Make your own decisions?" Bob shot back. "Lena, what are you saying? That would be chaos! Insanity! You cannot run a business with everyone just doing whatever they want!"

He was suddenly feeling very strange. He was perspiring for no obvious reason. His breathing was becoming shallow.

"That's not what I meant," Lena countered. "Again, I don't mean any disrespect. But it's chaotic *now* for that matter."

"And with no control, it would be even more chaotic! A disaster!" Bob said.

"I'm not saying there should be 'no control' – "

"SERVICE IS TOO SMALL!" someone said loudly, almost yelling.

Bob flinched. The voice was directly behind him. He felt surrounded – indeed was surrounded – and was inexplicably on the brink of panic.

It was Grumpy Gerald, whose notion of a conversational tone was akin to shouting. Bob whipped around to face him.

"THAT'S WHAT REALLY HONKS ME OFF!"

Bob abruptly felt a sharp stab of pain in his chest.

"I CAN HAVE TEN REPAIRS GOING ON AND I CAN'T LAY THEM OUT BECAUSE THERE'S NOT ENOUGH #!#^&@ SPACE!"*

"Why are you always swearing?" John demanded of Grumpy. "That's not right to the rest of us!"

"I'LL SAY WHATEVER THE HELL I WANT TO SAY!"

Bob swayed. He was losing his balance. The faces of all the workers around him were spinning, becoming a blur, as the pain in his chest became unbearable.

"Are you all right, Bob?" Lena asked.

No, Bob was not all right. He suddenly collapsed onto the floor.

"Oh!" Lena cried.

She knelt down next to him.

"I think ... I'm having ... a heart attack," Bob was barely able to murmur.

"Alice, call an ambulance!" Lena said. "John, go to the front entrance and let the ambulance people in when they arrive! Kevin, go get the first-aid kit and see if there's anything in it that might help! And Grumpy, don't you dare say another word!"

Chapter 3

In Which His Symptoms Mysteriously Vanish

However, as it happened, Bob was not having a heart attack. Once he was in the ambulance, he began feeling much better. When the ambulance arrived at the hospital, all of the symptoms had vanished. His shortness of breath, vertigo, chest pain had completely gone away.

"I'm fine," Bob announced. "I just need to get back to work."

"Not so fast," said Dr. Dibbs, his physician. "Something happened and we need to find out what."

"Meaning ... ?"

"We need to keep you here and run some tests."

"Keep me for how long?" Bob asked.

"Just a few days."

"A few *days?*"

"Yes, a few days at the most. We'll start right away. I'll order the tests as soon as you are admitted."

"But you don't understand!" said Bob. "My business won't run without me!"

"Why not?"

"It just won't! I have to be there! I have to make the decisions! I have to make sure things are getting done! I have to fix the problems when they occur!"

"Why can't your employees handle matters?" Dr. Dibbs asked.

"Because they're idiots!"

"Why are you hiring idiots?"

"I'm not!" said Bob. "In fact, some of them are very bright. But they just don't get it! They don't get the nuances. They don't understand the customers. They don't get the nitty gritty. They definitely don't get the big picture. Which is why I have to be there. Otherwise, all hell could break loose!"

"Well, that's a problem I can't solve," said Dr. Dibbs. "Mr. Bingham, if you want to sign yourself out against medical advice, that's up to you. We can't hold you prisoner. But a short while ago you were on the floor in intense pain gasping for air. You arrived here in an ambulance. Perhaps those facts should be important evidence that you might want to proceed cautiously."

Bob's wife, Emily, had been standing there listening the whole time. She now leaned forward and put her face directly in front of her husband's.

"Do ... what ... the doctor ... tells you," she said quietly and firmly.

And, reluctantly, Bob did.

*

The next few days were agonizing for Bob. At first, in between tests, he tried to stay in control of Burbells Universal by phone. But the main thing this accomplished was a spike in his anxiety levels. So while Bob was out of his hospital room enduring some procedure, Emily made his phone disappear.

She tried to feign ignorance when he returned to the room, but Bob knew what had happened.

"I want it back *now!*" he said.

"No. It's for your own good. You can have it back as soon as Dr. Dibbs releases you from the hospital."

"I could be bankrupt by then!"

"Too bad."

So, denied communication and information, Bob had nothing better to do than lie in his bed and worry about everything that was probably going wrong. He imagined one screw-up after another taking place. Foul-up after foul-up was no doubt happening and *they* wouldn't even know anything had gone afoul because they didn't know the business the way he did!

In Bob's view, none of them knew how to handle customers. Dealing with customers was something that only Bob did, because the employees didn't comprehend the likes and dislikes of one customer over another. Only Bob knew these things.

In his mind's eye, he saw disasters unfolding: Kevin mindlessly putting over-priced new inventory in all the wrong places, such that no one would ever find what they needed. Grumpy Gerald cussing away while swinging a sledgehammer at the walls of Service so as to widen his work area. John in Shipping rejecting all returns regardless of reason because he doesn't like to be inconvenienced by paperwork. Shy Alice performing her clerical duties with casual abandon – and ordering birthday cakes for everyone, heedless of the expense! And Lena rushing about hither and thither with her hair on fire after making unilateral decisions that would have terrible consequences.

A nurse now hurried into Bob's hospital room.

"Mr. Bingham, your blood pressure has gone sky high! It's two hundred over one-forty!"

"Am I having a heart attack?"

"Not yet," she said, "but soon!"

"Sorry. I've been thinking about my business. I have a lot that's bothering me."

She turned on the television for him.

"Watch some sports or a game show – anything to get your mind off your worries."

It had been years since Bob had watched television. He found a football game being broadcast and briefly became absorbed in it, in something that blissfully didn't matter very much, but he could not stay with it. There were too many issues bothering him.

High in the ranking of those issues was Lena. She was indeed the one employee he trusted to any degree. And he liked her as a person. Yet his mind kept flashing back to the meeting and her suggestion that the employees be allowed to make their own decisions and do their jobs as they saw fit. What rubbish! What a recipe for disaster! And even worse, Lena had made the suggestion *publicly*, in front of everyone! Granted, he had set up the meeting to hear suggestions, but Bob somehow felt betrayed.

*

After two days of tests, Dr. Dibbs and the hospital staff could find nothing physically wrong with Bob. Except that his cholesterol was high, his cardio was fine. Dr. Dibbs prescribed a statin for the cholesterol and suggested Bob get more exercise. As for what brought on the attack in the employee meeting, the diagnosis was "extreme anxiety". The cause? Undetermined.

Bob wondered about this. He remembered feeling a strange and intense fear, something like panic. *But why?* Bob wondered. What had brought on such groundless terror?

He had been in the middle, surrounded by everybody. Yes, *surrounded.* That was part of it. From what he could recall, the panic seemed to develop after he began to feel as if he might actually be under some kind of attack – an attack coming from all directions, from the workers with everyone making their mindless suggestions, and Bob in the middle, at the center, having to fend them off. It was almost as if he had had a pack of ravenous wolves all around him.

Of course he knew rationally that was not the case. But that was how it had *felt* to him – like wolves about to tear him apart. And then there was his trusted Lena telling him everybody should make their own decisions – like Bob's decisions weren't good enough – and that the company was chaotic. What a blow!

Well, it would be a long time until he would attempt communication with employees in that kind of meeting, Bob told himself.

*

The next morning, Bob received his official medical clearance to go home. But naturally he did not go straight home. He insisted that his wife Emily, who was driving, take him to Burbells Universal. Emily knew better than to argue.

Bob had not for one second believed that everything would be "fine" during his absence. His concern was, how bad would it be?

He had a dark fantasy that he would arrive at Burbells Universal and the entire building would be a pile of smoking rubble. No, of course that was extremely unlikely, but nevertheless ...

When he saw that the building was still standing, he was not at all surprised, but he did wonder what would be the hidden damage inside. He thanked Emily and sent her on her way, saying he would catch a ride home one way or another.

Inside, instead of his dire imaginings, Bob found a quiet atmosphere. Nothing was on fire, certainly not Lena's hair. But the quietude seemed almost eerie.

Lena was the first to notice him.

"Bob! You're back!"

She immediately went to him and embraced him. Everyone then broke into applause.

Bob was touched. He never expected any of them to care one way or another whether he lived or died.

"Thank you! Thank you all so much!" Bob told them. "Now, back to work!"

He turned to Lena.

"How is everything going?"

"Well, all right, I guess. We're doing the best we can, doing as much as we can do," she said. "I've been keeping a list of decisions that need to be made, questions that have come up, problems that need to be solved ... "

Lena picked up her list, which was several pages long.

"Should we go through everything? Or do you need some time to yourself?"

"No, let's just dive right into it," Bob said. "Come into my office."

As they went through the list, Bob found himself becoming irritated that so many things had stalled and were not finished even when the decisions to be made were small and petty.

"Lena, I fail to see why you couldn't have decided this," he said of one issue. "I mean, it's not that complicated!"

"True," said Lena, "but not long ago on something very similar, I did make the call without asking you and you were grouchy all afternoon. Turned out you knew something I didn't. So I figured that, rather than make a mistake, it was better to wait for you to return."

"But, Lena, this time I was in the hospital! Surely you could have taken a chance in the interest of getting an order out the door!"

"And what if I was wrong in your opinion?"

"All right, all right. Let's just get things moving again."

"I'm very glad you were gone for only a couple of days," Lena said. "Just imagine, if you were gone for a month, we'd have to shut down."

Bob glared at her.

"You're being sarcastic," he said.

"No, Bob, I'm serious."

"Fine. What's next?"

Chapter 4

Moe

The next day, the DynaMicro-512 was acting up again and Bob was trying to recalibrate it when he noticed at the edge of his vision a tall, gaunt man with white hair who had approached and was standing nearby. Bob hardly needed to turn his head to know who it was.

"Hello, Moe."

The thin lips on the face of Maurice Strickett curled into a dis-humorous smile.

"Hello, Bob."

"What brings you here?"

"You do."

"I didn't call you."

"Of course not. But I've been hearing snippets of news about you ... and I am concerned about my investment."

"Hearing? Snippets?"

"About your recent health issues."

"Not sure what you mean."

"Your nervous breakdown," said Moe.

"Oh, that! No, I would hardly call it a nervous breakdown. Nothing like that at all. It was minor! Very minor. I mean, here I am just a few days later! Productive! At the top of my game!"

"Really, Bob? Top of your game? This is it? This is as good as it gets? As good as *you* get?"

Quietly, after glancing over his shoulder to see if anyone was listening, Bob said, "I'm trying, Moe. I'm really trying."

"I'm sure. Someplace private where we can talk?"

Bob gestured toward his office. Moe led the way.

"You said you were concerned about your investment," Bob said as he closed his office door.

"Yes. I made a substantial investment in this company and I have yet to see a substantial return. Meanwhile the market has been growing nicely. However, Burbells Universal does not seem to be able to take advantage of that market expansion."

"Moe, I'm sure it's just a matter of time."

"That's what you've said in the past. But time ... well, has passed. No improvement has materialized."

"I'm doing everything I can, Moe. There is no one who has given more to this company – to this business, even to this industry – than I have."

"I don't doubt that, Bob."

"I'm working something like eighty hours a week, Moe! I'm not exaggerating!"

"Bob, I really don't care if you work ten hours a week or one hundred hours a week. If you can work ten hours a week – or ten hours a month, for that matter – and keep the bottom line improving, that's preferable to working eighty hours a week and not be getting anywhere."

"Honestly, I don't know what more I can do."

"Then maybe you should step aside."

Bob was stunned.

"That stings, Moe. It stings and it stinks. It's a slap in the face. And, no, I will not step aside. I've put everything I've got into this company. More than you know. Including my life. Almost."

"What do you mean?"

"Never mind. The important thing is that I am not quitting. And you can't force me. I have the majority of equity in this enterprise. You are a minority investor. So I have control; you don't. And there is nothing you can do about it."

"Uh-huh."

"Sales may not be growing – though actually they are growing a little, just not at a rate to your liking – but by the same token we're not going under."

"You're treading water," Moe said. "That's all you're doing."

"Better to tread water than to drown, don't you think?"

"For how long? How long can you and this company tread water? A market is never static. Technology, competitors, customers – none of these are static. If your business is not growing you are falling behind. I repeat the question: how long do you think you can tread water? And if all you're doing is staying in one place, just getting by, at eighty hours a week, for however long, what's the point?"

"When I figure it out, I'll let you know."

"Listen to me. I think that at the core you are a winner, Bob. Seriously. You have the right stuff inside to be a winner. But you don't know how. You don't know how to apply yourself in a winning way. You're not getting it done. That makes you a loser."

"You are so full of – "

"I walked in a few minutes ago. And what were you doing? You were fixing a piece of equipment."

"Well, what's wrong with that? It has to be done!"

"By you?"

"Why not me? I know how to fix the problem!"

"But why couldn't the operator fix it?"

"He doesn't know how!"

"And why doesn't he?"

"Because it would take *a lot* of training before he was experienced enough to be competent. And I can fix the problem in half an hour, maybe less."

"Why not call in a service technician?"

"That costs money! And time! I doubt we could even get a service tech for that equipment on the same day we called. I can get it done for no extra cost in a fraction of the time!"

"Really? Doesn't cost anything if you do it? Tell me, Bob, what is *not* getting done while you are doing the fixing?"

"What are you talking about?"

"You have a lot of responsibilities, just as every business owner and every executive does. So while you're taking half an hour to fix this machine, something else is not getting done. Right?"

Bob did not answer.

"Here's the big question," says Moe. "It's a career question. Are you a leader or are you a fixer?"

After blinking his eyes a few times, Bob said, "Well ... I suppose I'm both."

"No, I think you're a fixer. And I'll tell you something else. The reason you work these eighty-hour weeks, aside from proving how essential you are, is because you're always having to play catch-up on everything you're not getting done while you're farting around fixing something."

Bob crossed his arms over his chest.

"That's enough, Moe. I am sick of your insults. Tell me what *the hell* you want by coming here – so that I can get back to fixing or whatever *I think* needs to be done in *my* company."

"All right, I'll cut to the chase," said Moe. "My patience with you has turned out to be not a virtue. I put in a lot of money; I'm getting not much back. But I'll give you one last chance, Bob. I'll give you six months."

"Six months to do what?"

"To show improvement. To show me that you can do more with this company than just tread water. I'm not expecting miracles, but I am expecting clear signs of ongoing, sustainable improvement. I want to see sales increasing and evidence that they will continue to increase. I want to see more customer accounts. I especially want to see stronger net income – shall we say *robust* income growth or at least solid signs of it. And I want to see some of those profits going into my pocket. I want to see lower costs. I want to see throughput increasing, more inventory turns, better end-to-end flow, customers who are thrilled to do business with us. In short, improvement!"

"You think I don't want those things myself, Moe? I do! And I will do my best! As always!"

"I don't want 'your best.' I want you to get it done."

"Or ... ?"

"Or you're out."

"My goodness gracious!" said Bob, sarcasm dripping everywhere. "That really does sound like an ultimatum. How could that be?"

"Because it is an ultimatum."

"Wait a minute, Moe. You cannot do anything to me. Not legally. You're a silent partner. You took your chance, as did I. By contract agreement, you can't push me out."

"I will find a way. One way or another. Six months. Deliver or you are out."

Bob stared at Moe.

"So I will now take my leave and allow you to go about fixing whatever. And, seriously, I do hope you figure out how you're going to meet my challenge."

Moe stepped toward Bob's office door, opened it, then paused and looked back.

"You want a suggestion?" Moe asked. "Why don't you cut back to sixty hours a week. You might get more accomplished."

*

Shortly after Moe left, Lena walked in. Bob was staring into space.

"Excuse me, Bob, but the DynaMicro still isn't calibrated and Felix is wondering what he should do."

Bob started to spring from his seat so as to run and fix the problem, but managed to stop himself and sit back down again.

"Tell Felix to figure it out and fix it himself," Bob said.

"I'm sorry, but Felix doesn't have the first clue about fixing it. There is no way he can figure it out on his own. All he knows is how to press the buttons in the right sequence and then follow the instructions on the screen."

"All right, all right. Tell him I'll be there in a minute."

"If I may ask, is everything okay? I saw Moe leaving ... "

"Moe has become threatening. And, Lena, that's strictly between you and me."

"In what way is he threatening?"

"I'd rather not say. But I think he's serious. He's going to make trouble. Not now, but eventually."

"Trouble? In what way?"

Bob waved his hand in the air as if to dissipate a bad odor. Then, all but ignoring her question, he said, "He's an odd character, Moe is. I'm sorry our paths ever crossed. Yet, thinking about what he said to me, I have to admit he has a valid point or two."

"What does he want?"

"Improvement!" Bob said. "Don't we all!"

Now he did stand.

"Well," he said, "back to it."

Bob went to the machine at issue and beckoned to Felix.

"I want you to learn," Bob said. "This will be lesson number one in recalibrating a DynaMicro-512. The first thing to do ... "

So he began to teach Felix.

Chapter 5

The Howitzers

Having walked Felix through the recalibration process – hoping that problem might be permanently solved – Bob turned his attention to his own list of tasks. Then Lena came in to ask a few questions, and when she did, Bob mentally noted that most of the answers should have been obvious.

"Lena, why do you need to ask me these things?"

"Because I want to be absolutely certain that I know what you want."

"But you generally do know what I expect. You're not like the others who have to be told every little thing."

"May I speak plainly?" she asked.

"Please do."

"Beyond basic everyday routines, nobody here has any confidence that if they were to take the initiative what they do will meet with your approval. They are afraid they'll be second-guessed, spoken to, or even reprimanded. So they do nothing until they can get your instructions and input."

"Seriously?"

"Yes. You do it all the time."

"Do what?"

"You insist on being involved in everything. And when you're involved, you take over. You're the owner and you're a perfectionist. So everybody has to defer to you."

"Well, isn't that my privilege? Yes, I *am* the owner. And I do admit that I am a perfectionist."

"You may have that privilege," said Lena, "but how is that helping the business?"

Bob shut his eyes and pinched the bridge of his nose.

"Listen," he said, "there are a lot of complexities in this industry. And I am often the only one in this company who knows how to deal with those complexities. What am I to do?"

"Simplify," said Lena.

"That's easy to say, but difficult to accomplish! Where do I even start?"

Lena shrugged her shoulders. Bob shook his head.

"It *is* disturbing," he said, "that I am gone just a couple of days and I come back to a list of questions and problems as long as my arm."

"If I could read your mind from a distance and know exactly what you wanted," said Lena, "I daresay that I could have handled most of those issues while you were gone."

"But Lena, there are instances when even I don't know what I want! I have to think and make a decision and then convey it to everyone else! And, meanwhile, Moe is demanding growth. I can't keep up with what we have going now!"

"Can't keep up? Bob, it's amazing to me that you're able to handle as much as you do."

"What's that supposed to mean?"

"Look at everything you're involved in," she said. "First, marketing and sales."

"But I know all the customers! I know their individual preferences! Unfortunately, nobody else does."

"Next, accounting and payroll."

"Well, of course! Who else?"

"And finance."

"Lena, banks deal with owners and top managers. I can't change that."

"Plus purchasing. When Kevin can't find thera-mods, you're the one on the phone tracking down a new supply."

"Well, I had to jump in – it was a crisis!"

"I've seen you do the same thing many, many times," she said. "You jump in and then you take over."

"Because I want to make sure we get the best possible price."

"And only you can do that?"

"Lena, I'm becoming a little annoyed by this discussion."

"You also step in to prioritize the workflow and the sequence of orders."

"Because that goes hand in hand with sales! I know the customers and some customers are content to wait longer for delivery while others need fulfillment *right now*!"

"In addition," she continued, "you handle custom designs and special orders."

"But that is something I really enjoy!"

"How about maintenance? You're involved in that as well."

"Now wait. I just trained Felix to do the recalibration of the DynaMicro. So I shouldn't be involved in that anymore."

"My point remains, Bob, that you're involved in just about everything – and you won't let go."

"Lena, a small business owner must wear a lot of hats. It's a matter of necessity."

"All I am saying is that it's no wonder you're ready to hang yourself."

This struck Bob and hurt him. His face took on the look of a sad young boy – which melted Lena's heart.

"I'm sorry, Bob. I should not have said that."

"Actually, it's true. I am overwhelmed. And I don't know what to do about it."

At that moment, Bob's phone rang. He looked at the screen and groaned.

"It's Henrie," he said. "I have to take this."

*

Henrietta Howitzer was president and CEO of the company HTI – High Trajectory Innovations. She was married to and in business with Henry Howitzer, who was executive chairman of HTI. Husband Henry Howitzer had the management skills of a chimpanzee, but was a phenomenal salesman (at least by his own account). Wife Henrie, however, ran the show.

Until recently, HTI had been Bob's company's biggest customer. That was until HTI went from being "slow pay" to "no pay". They owed a lot of money to Burbells Universal.

"Hello, Henrie," Bob answered in a listless tone.

"Hello, Bob!" she said brightly.

"How may I help you?"

"I'm glad you asked, Bob! Listen, my husband, Henry, just closed a magnificent sale with ... well, I can't reveal the buyer's name, but you would know it instantly if I told you. We're talking *big*, Bob. Really big. Huge."

"I see. Henri, excuse me, I happen to have my operations manager, Lena Novak, here in my office and I'd like to bring her into the conversation. Let me put you on speaker."

He pressed the icon.

"Hello, Mrs. Howitzer! This is Lena."

"Hello, Lena. I've been telling Bob that HTI just closed a monumental piece of business. And we'd like to start fulfillment right away. So I would like to place an immediate order for five thousand units of your BU-Fifty-Two model. Of course, you would give us your best volume discount. How soon could we take delivery?"

"Um," said Bob, "that depends. Of course we would love the business. But how would HTI be paying for the order?"

"What do you mean?" asked Henrie.

"Would HTI be paying in advance? With, you know, cash?"

"Heavens no! Of course not! We would need credit!"

"Um, Henrie, I'm not sure," said Bob.

"Why? Bob, listen! Those five thousand units, that's just the beginning! You will be amazed at the orders we'll be placing in the future! So, we need credit! And here's the icing on the cake. HTI will be purchasing one hundred percent of our burbell supply needs from you, Bob, for the duration of the project! You will have an *exclusive!*"

"An exclusive? Meaning that we would be the sole supplier?"

"Yes! Isn't that exciting! You'll be making money hand over fist!"

"Henrie, thank you for thinking of us. And I must say that it all sounds interesting. But HTI already owes us a lot of money. And you haven't been paying."

"Oh? Really? I wasn't aware of that."

"Well, it's true."

"Listen Bob, here at HTI, we've been strategically positioning ourselves to be *the* number-one purveyor of burbell applications. And it's paying off! If you haven't been receiving payments – "

"We haven't, Henrie. And I've tried to get through to you several times."

"That's because we're *so* busy! Any lack of payments, well, it's something that just slipped through the cracks. But this new contract is so lucrative, we'll have our credit bill paid down in no time. And it's a multi-year contract, you know."

"Is it? Henrie, how much business are we actually talking about?"

"I'm not at liberty to say exactly. But I assure you the amount is quite large."

"In the millions?" Bob asked.

"Again, I'm not at liberty to reveal those numbers. But Bob ... you can imagine!"

"Yes, yes, I can imagine."

"Excuse me, Mrs. Howitzer, but it would help immensely to have some idea of the actual numbers," said Lena, "so that we can plan appropriately."

"I've told you I cannot reveal exact figures! Listen though! This *initial* order for five thousand units that I'd like to place right now, today, is just the beginning! Five thousand! That should tell you something!"

"Yes, perhaps it does, Henrie," said Bob. "Even so, it would be absolutely terrific if we could get some kind of payment for the units already delivered to HTI – let's say fifty percent of the outstanding balance?"

"Oh, now, Bob. I don't think we could do that," she said. "HTI must preserve its financial resources in order to fulfill this enormous contract. And I would hate for you to miss out on this opportunity. You have always been our preferred supplier."

"I appreciate that, Henrie. However, we have cashflow needs of our own here."

"Then I suppose HTI will just have to approach your competitors to see if one or more of them can accommodate us."

"Now hold on, Henrie. Let me think this through. It's late in the day and I have several obligations I have to conclude. But allow me to sleep on it and I'll get back to you in the morning."

"Well ... all right," she said. "I just hope you make the smart decision."

Henrie ended the call. Bob looked at Lena.

"So let's say I was still in the hospital and unreachable. Lena, if you had to make the decision, what would your decision be? Take the order on credit or walk away?"

Lena shook her head.

"I don't know, Bob. If she's on the up-and-up about the contract and how lucrative it is, then it would be short-sighted, even stupid, not to go along on her terms. And HTI *is* our biggest account."

"They were until they quit paying."

"Yes, and it is rather puzzling why she wouldn't offer at least some kind of payment, maybe twenty percent or something, against the outstanding balance," Lena said. "And why is she being so secretive about the contract details?"

"I don't know," said Bob. "But she's offering – potentially – a lot of business and a lot of money."

"So, if you don't mind my asking, what *are* you going to do?"

"I'm going to do what I said. I'm going to sleep on it and hope the right answer comes to me in the morning."

*

Bob as usual worked into the evening, well past the end of the work day. When he got home, Emily was as usual sullen.

"The kids and I have already eaten," she said coldly. "I did save something for you if you want it."

"Of course I want it," said Bob.

She sat at the kitchen table while he ate in silence.

"You seem troubled," Emily said.

"I'm always troubled."

"So what are tonight's troubles?"

"Something I remember. I wouldn't say this is at the top of my 'trouble' list, but when I was being admitted to the hospital I was telling Dr. Dibbs that my business couldn't run without me. Which I think is true. And he asked why my employees couldn't handle matters while I was away."

"Yes, I remember," said Emily. "You told him they couldn't manage on their own because, using your words, 'they're idiots.' Then he asked – "

"Why am I hiring idiots? Well, Emily, I'm not intentionally hiring idiots. They just turn out that way."

"Oh, Bob. You don't have a clue, do you."

"Perhaps not, but I am going to have to get a clue and figure this out, because the wolves are at the company door, so to speak. Moe Strickett is demanding dividends for his investment and the only way to give him what he wants is to increase sales and profits.

"And just today our biggest customer – once upon a time the biggest, until they quit paying us – called and offered a huge order, but only if we would offer additional credit. Emily, I don't know what to do. Moe wants profits. The company could use the business. But they haven't been paying. Obviously, it's risky, but – "

He stopped because Emily had reached across the table and placed her hand on Bob's forearm. It was the first affection she had shown him in quite some time. He reached across to her.

"Come here," he said.

She came around the corner of the table, sat in his lap, and hugged him.

Chapter 6

The Dream Tree

That night, as Bob slept next to Emily, he had a strange dream. He dreamed he was at work. Which was not unusual. But this dream was far more vivid and disturbing.

In the dream, he was wandering about inside the company building and everything at first felt normal and benign. He was seeking something, but he did not know what. And whatever it was, he did not know where to find it. So he was moving about, directionless.

He became aware that there were other people around him. He felt their presence, but at first did not know who they were. Then some partially recognizable faces emerged in the fog of the dream. They were his employees, some of them. Others were just random people – the undertaker who was going to handle Bob's funeral was one. Still others were just semi-human. They had mechanical aspects attached to their biological bodies.

At first, Bob did not feel threatened by these dream people and bizarre cyber creatures. All seemed well. Then suddenly it wasn't. They – whoever they were – had started a fire. Orange flames licked at the walls. And nobody seemed to be terribly concerned, nobody except Bob, who was shouting, but was being unheard or ignored. A tiny bucket of water appeared in Bob's hands. He tried to run toward the fire in an attempt to put it out, but though he was trying with everything he had, he was barely moving – and by the time he reached the fire the bucket was empty.

Bob turned one way and another. All around were fires and dense black smoke. And nobody else in the dream seemed to care.

Then Lena was there.

"Help me put out the fires!" Bob implored.

But she didn't seem to understand.

"Start climbing," she said.

"Climb?"

"Out of this."

"Out of what?"

She didn't answer because she was gone, vanished.

Bob began searching for her – or once more searching for something unnameable and unknown. Then he found the tree.

He was in his office and there was his desk in front of him. And right out of his desk, right out of the middle of it, a big tree had grown. The trunk went up and up, through the ceiling and seemingly onward to the sky.

"Start climbing!"

Whose voice was calling? Was it his own? An inner voice? Lena's voice? Emily's? All of those? He didn't know. But Bob got on top of his desk and began to climb. At first, he didn't seem to be getting anywhere. He would climb so far, then he would slip back. But at last he gained some height. The climbing got easier and faster. He went up and up and up.

"Look!" one of those voices suggested.

Bob looked out and indeed there was a beautiful world out there. It was full of colors – greens and blues and reds and golds and oranges – fabulous colors in fabulous shapes. He so very much wanted to be in that colorful, incredible world. So he took a step toward it, reaching out with his arm and hand.

Then he suddenly realized that the tree had begun to sway back and forth. Bob looked down. They were down there – whoever they were. They were people he recognized somewhat, though they were zombie-like. And there were the human machines, part flesh and part techno assembly. Plus, there were the beastie-folk with their bear-like hides and wolverine teeth.

They were attacking the tree, destroying it, cutting it down with saws or even teeth. And nobody seemed to know or care that Bob was in the tree, way up high.

There was a loud and terrible *crack.* The tree began to fall. Bob felt himself plunging. Down and down and down.

Bob began to yell in his sleep – only to have no sound come from this mouth. He was thrashing this way and that, in a futile attempt to save himself inside the horrific dream, the dream gone bad.

"Bob! Bob!" Emily was saying as she nudged her husband to awaken him.

His eyes sprung open.

"You were tossing and turning like you were going to die," Emily said.

"Well, I was going to die. In my nightmare."

"What? Who?"

"Nothing, never mind," he said. "I'm sorry I woke you. Try to go back to sleep."

She did, but Bob could not.

Unable to sleep, he stared into the darkness. He tried to make rational sense of the dream – almost always a futile exercise – but just as he was at last about to drift off, something clicked inside his mind and in astonishment he sat straight up in bed.

The dream seemed to have elements of truth to it. As in the dream, he seemed every day to be wandering from task to task, crisis to crisis, while the people he employed, people he was paying, seemed disengaged, apathetic. There were fires breaking out and the people were powerless to put them out or even prevent them.

Then there was the tree growing out of his desk in the middle of his office and a disembodied voice telling him to climb. Like the only way out was up. But once he got high enough that he had some perspective, he saw the whole world out there and it was richly colored and vibrant. Bob wanted to be there again, in a place where he could look out and see everything. Yet below were the fires and the smoke and the zombie-like people and all the chaos that could destroy the tree. How could he control all or any of that? The dream may have given him some images and sounds that suggested the truth, but the dream was not a solution.

"I have to find that for myself," he murmured.

Bob finally managed to sleep and it seemed that as soon as he did, the clock on his phone was bleeping its infernal alarm, rousing him at dawn. Then Bob did something he had never done, not in recent memory at least. He put the phone in silent mode and fell back to sleep.

*

When he awakened, Bob dragged himself out of bed and was shocked at the hour. He entered Burbells Universal around 9:30 a.m., which was unheard of. Even as he came through the door, he was fretting over what the extreme luxury of sleeping in might have cost him. Lena was clearly relieved to see him.

"Where have you been, Bob? I've been calling and calling, trying to reach you!"

"Oh nuts," he said. "I put my phone in silent mode and forgot to switch it back. It's no wonder I've been in such a good mood!"

"I'm afraid it won't last," said Lena. "I've got bad news ... and more bad news."

Bob already had his phone out and was scrolling through the list of missed calls.

"Uh-huh," he said absently. "Well, why don't you give me the bad news first."

"Felix got hit by a bus."

"Seriously? How?"

"Well," said Lena, holding up one hand, "let's say this is Felix."

She made a fist with her other hand.

"And this is the bus. And *boom!*"

She smashed her fist into the palm of the hand representing Felix.

"Oh no!" said Bob. "When?"

"This morning."

"Is he alive?"

"Yes. He's in the hospital in serious condition," said Lena. "I'm going to pick up a sympathy card on my lunch break. We'll all sign it and send it to Felix."

"Good idea. Very thoughtful."

"But there is more bad news."

"What?"

"Without Felix there is no one to operate the DynaMicro. Except for Kevin. He says he knows how to run it. But I didn't want to put him on the DynaMicro until I had your permission."

Bob tipped his head back and gaped at the ceiling.

"Yes, by all means, put Kevin on the DynaMicro right away," he told her. "I've got calls to make."

*

At the top of his call list was Henrie Howitzer. He could not afford to ignore her. Bob was silently rehearsing what he was going to say to Henrie, when Lena came in.

"Kevin is setting up the machine," she said. "And here's your coffee. I warmed it up in the microwave."

"Thank you," he said.

"If you don't mind my asking, have you made a decision about HTI?" she asked.

"Yes. I'm going to accept Henrie's order on credit terms."

"I hope it's a good call."

"Me too."

"Mind if I ask how you came to that choice?" Lena asked. "I'm just trying to learn."

Bob chuckled.

"Lena, I'm not sure you ought to be learning from the Bob Bingham School of Management," he said. "I am painfully aware that my methods are probably not eligible for business 'best practices' status. Many of my decisions spring as much from the gut as from the brain. Perhaps I should be running some sophisticated computer analysis to tell me if the Howitzers will pay their bill or not. But there is no time for that. All I have to rely upon is my gut instinct and some basic logic."

"But still, Bob, why this choice?"

"Reason number one: Moe Strickett. Moe wants growth. This order from Henrie will definitely move the needle. Moe should be happy and maybe he'll get off my back."

"Yes, but extending to HTI even more credit when they haven't been paying ... ? Sounds to me like trouble."

"True. But there is risk either way. You picked up on that yesterday, Lena. There is opportunity risk. If I take a hard line and insist upon cash payment, then Henrie walks away and we miss the opportunity to profit from what might well be a very big deal. Her blowhard husband, Henry, has indeed been known to close some lucrative sales. And if wife Henrie walks, we still won't get our money. We'd have to take legal action to collect, or just write it off. Both of those are ugly.

"On the other hand, there is financial risk. If I extend additional credit to HTI and Henrie yet again does not pay – or does not pay enough, soon enough – then we are in a serious bind. This firm could be sucked into a financial black hole from which we might not escape."

"Bob, are you sure you want to take this risk?

"No, I'm not sure. But then, there must be a reason why HTI wants five thousand units. I mean, you don't order in that kind of quantity just for the fun of it. To one extent or another, the demand has to be real. Most of our sales are small to medium. This is the first huge order in a long time. So I'm taking it and hoping for the best."

He took a sip of his coffee.

"Of course," he added, "*hope* is another of those four-letter words."

"As is *luck*. And *love*."

"Yes, better those than some others."

"Bob, I'd better get to work," said Lena. "You're going to call Henrie this morning?"

"In a few minutes."

"Let me know what we should do. We'll have to order extra parts and materials for an order that large."

He drank his coffee for a moment, then picked up his phone.

"Hello, Henrie! It's Bob Bingham! How are you this morning? Listen, I've thought about our discussion yesterday, and I've decided to move forward with you. I just need a few clarifications ... "

Chapter 7

The Airport

An hour later, Bob was across town meeting with Rupert, the HTI purchasing manager. Bob emphasized – as he had when speaking to Henrie on the phone earlier – that Burbells Universal must have payment in a timely fashion. Bob did not use threats about withholding delivery or about anything else. He simply stated firmly his expectations and hoped it would be enough. Rupert assured him that prompt payment would not be a problem. Thus assured and with a copy of his purchase order in hand, Bob returned.

As soon as Bob returned to Burbells Universal, he could sense something was wrong. And indeed there was.

"What happened?" he asked Lena.

"Well, with your approval, Kevin began operating the DynaMicro. Turns out he was a bit overconfident of his abilities."

"Oh, no! What happened? He ... ?"

"He made some mistakes," said Lena. "The machine got out of control. As a result, the DynaMicro has to be – "

"Recalibrated," Bob finished.

"Yes. And with Felix having been hit by a bus, there is nobody else who can do the recalibration ... "

"Except me!" said Bob. *"Arrgh!"*

"I'm sorry. But who could have predicted it?"

"Yes. All right, all right."

*

Bob set aside everything else he had to do, went to the DynaMicro-512 and got to work – all but praying that Moe Strickett wouldn't unexpectedly show up and make his usual insulting remarks. And of course, just as Bob was about to test the recalibration, in walked Moe.

"I can see you haven't learned a thing since my last visit," Moe said.

"That is not true!" Bob countered – instantly angry at his white-haired antagonist. "I personally trained the main operator of this machine, as you suggested."

"Then where is he?"

"He got hit by a bus."

"Oh. Sorry. Too bad. Well, why did you train just one person? In any company, there is always employee turnover, promotions, changing assignments – and sick days. So, for that matter, why not train everybody, given that this device seems to be so crucial?"

"*Everybody?* I can't train everybody! The time, the cost – it would be prohibitive!"

"Can't say that your personal involvement right now is boosting profits, now can you?"

"Moe, I absolutely must get this machine up and running. And *you* are slowing me down."

"All right, I'll be quick about it. By the end of the month, which is coming up soon, I want to see updated financial reports."

Bob was immediately suspicious.

"Financial reports? What do you mean?"

"You know, Bob! Financial reports! You're a business owner, aren't you? Spreadsheets. With numbers. Lots and lots of numbers."

"Of course I know! But why do you want to see them?"

"Because I'm your partner and I have a right to look at the books. And, ah, someone on my staff noticed that you have not been keeping current with your records. You know, I'll take the blame on that one. Even I am not perfectly oversightful on everything. But I do want to see the current numbers – and I want to see the reports regularly. I don't understand why they fell off the way that they have."

"All right," said Bob. "Nothing to worry about."

"Good. Because I might want to see if there is any fraud going on."

"*Fraud?* That's ridiculous! You know me. I'm an honorable man. I would never do such a thing."

"Well, I do hope so," said Moe. "But one can never rule it out, can one? Besides, this would be a good time to set some baselines for the sake of future measurement – so that down the road, we can tell if this business is really improving or not."

"Yes. Okay. Fine. I'll get your damned financial reports for you. Not like we don't have better things to do!"

Moe slowly shook his head, but he smiled at Bob with a sympathetic expression.

"I was more-or-less kidding about the 'fraud' stuff, Bob. Listen, the numbers are your friends – even when you hate what they look like. *Especially* when you hate what the numbers look like. This is ultimately for your benefit, Bob. For everybody's benefit."

"Right. It doesn't feel beneficial, Moe, not when I have everything else to do."

Moe checked the time.

"I'd like you to come with me," he said to Bob. "Won't take long. Half an hour at the most."

"Moe, I'm trying to finish this critical adjustment! I have to get this machine running!"

"All right. Go ahead and finish. I'll wait."

Bob wrapped up the recalibration in fairly short order.

"Where are we going?" he asked Moe.

"I want to show you something."

*

The two men left the building and got into Moe's car, an exotic vehicle with sleek lines that suggested speed and sophistication. As he drove, Moe was apparently thinking and said nothing at first. Then ...

"Let me ask you an important question, Bob. What does Burbells Universal make?"

"As you know, Moe, we make burbells."

"True. But what is the underlying, all-essential thing the company must make?

"Is this a trick question?"

"No – and yes."

"Um ... well, we must make burbells so as to compete in the burbells market. And we sell burbell-related services. Design services. Maintenance and repair services. But everything we do is all about burbells and their many valuable applications."

"Sorry, Bob, but that is not what your company – our company – needs to make."

"I'm not following you."

"This company of ours needs to make money."

"Obviously!"

"Burbells are the means to that end, the means of making money. That is foremost and essential for every business."

"Moe, that's a hard-nosed way of putting it."

"Yes, it is. And I have one of the hardest noses of all the people I know."

"Just seems to me that the company's purpose should be something more idealistic."

"Well," said Moe, "I'm not saying a business shouldn't have ideals and be idealistic. On the contrary, to my way of thinking, a business *should* have ideals and *should* be idealistic – or at least be true to its values. But the infrastructure of that idealism is money – revenue, income, cash in the bank, investments for the future. Put succinctly, the business has to make money."

The car slowed and eased toward the curb. Bob recognized that they were quite near the one of the city's airports.

"And if the business is not making money," Moe continued, "then all your idealism isn't worth a damn. Do you read me, Bob?"

"Yes, I get it."

The car was now parked.

"Let's walk for a bit," said Moe.

They got out. There was a rising roar – a jet aircraft spooling up its engines for takeoff. A moment later, the plane came into sight as it gathered speed on the runway and then rose into the air. Moe waited for the roar to subside.

"Bob, do you know how many businesses I own?"

"A few."

"I own seven. Four of them I own outright. And I have a significant stake in three others, one of them being Burbells Universal. I used to own or have an interest in eleven businesses. But I found that was too many and I sold the less desirable ones, keeping the best while always looking for new opportunities."

"How can you manage so many?" Bob asked.

"I don't. They manage themselves."

"Manage themselves?"

"Yes. For the most part."

"Can't say that I've ever heard of a self-managing business."

"Bob, I don't mean that they are on autopilot. The people inside those businesses do the managing. As the owner, I stay out of the way as far as day-to-day operations – though I do pay attention. If I see events that are taking a company in the wrong direction, or if I see an opportunity that could send the business in a better direction, then I do step in. Otherwise, I leave them alone."

They came to a bench overlooking the airport runway. Moe gestured for them to sit down.

"These businesses I own," Moe said, "they're each different from the next. One is a retailer. Another is a finance company. A third does management consulting. But I think of them as being much the same at the core. Do you know how I think of them?"

Bob shrugged his shoulders.

"Money machines," said Moe. "That's how I look at them. Each business is a money machine. Each one sits there and runs and runs and runs reliably, year after year, and over time it earns a lot of money – for its managers, for its employees, for the community and the nation through taxes, and for me. This does a lot of good for a lot of people."

"I don't doubt that it does," said Bob.

"That's my vision for Burbells Universal, for it to become a reliable, high-quality machine that makes money and does excellent work. Are you in agreement? Can you share that vision?"

"Yes, Moe, I can see what you're driving at."

"You can have your ideals and you should. But you cannot achieve them unless you can pay for them."

The jet whine began again. They watched the aircraft come charging down the runway and lift off into the sky.

"Did you see the name on that plane that just took off? Sunn Airlines, started by its current CEO, James Sunn. He's a good friend of mine. Very successful, both himself as a top manager and the business as well. But, if I may make a point, Bob, you don't see Mr. Sunn piloting each of his planes. You don't see him supervising the aircraft maintenance or working in baggage claim or anything like that. Jimmy Sunn stays removed from all that. He stands back. He takes in the big picture, while others do what they were hired to do. That's what you have to do, Bob. You have to stand back."

Moe stood up, as did Bob.

"I may be hard-nosed, Bob, but I am not hard-hearted. I continue to want you to succeed. You're a good engineer. All you have to do is engineer for us a business that will grow and become increasingly valuable and vital. Can you do it? I'm waiting to find out."

Chapter 8

Time Traps

Moe dropped Bob at the entrance of Burbells Universal.

"How about next week, say Friday?" Moe asked as Bob was getting out of the car.

"For what?"

"For me to review the numbers," he said. "Friday, at ten o'clock?"

"Good enough."

"See you then, if not sooner," said Moe. "Too-da-loo!"

The sleek car drove away. Bob stood at the entrance, then pivoted and walked away. He needed some time to himself. Time to think. He walked as he thought about what Moe had said at the airport.

Bob was genuinely intrigued. A self-managing, reliable money machine? Was such a thing even possible? The "self-managing" part was especially interesting. There were many parts of his work life that he hated, but at the top of the list was hands-on management.

It seemed almost funny to Bob that five years ago, when he had started the business, management had not seemed as though it would be very difficult. Just tell people what to do and make sure they did what they were told, he had reasoned. How complicated could that be?

Now, half a decade later, it was very complicated. So many things tended to go amiss. So much seemed to require Bob's constant and personal attention. And there were all the aggravations, small and large – employees not communicating with each other, customers turning fickle, inventory not matching sales orders, equipment breakdowns, etc., etc.

Yet Moe had an interest in how many businesses? *Seven?* Obviously, Moe was not doing much hands-on management, if any at all. Indeed, Moe had claimed that his money-machine companies managed themselves. Well, wouldn't that be nice! But was that even possible? Could it really work? *How* could it work?

Knowing hard-nosed Moe as he did, Bob believed that his silent partner probably was not making an idle boast. There was probably truth to it.

Then there was Moe's challenge for Bob to "engineer" the business. Bob began to wonder. If he could engineer the perfect company – or a more perfect company than the one he had now – what would it be like? What would be its characteristics? Its components? Its culture?

Popping into Bob's mind was the analogy of an engine. Turn on the engine and it runs. Simple as that. Give the engine fuel and periodic maintenance and it should run reliably for many years – and without constant technical fiddling by the owner. Why couldn't his company run like that?

If such a thing was possible, what would it be like? What characteristics might it have? How could he achieve it?

He shook his head. No. Burbells Universal was so far from being self-managing that the notion seemed ridiculous. Every day, it seemed, there was a crisis – often more than one. So much could happen and there could be such bad outcomes. He could not, at this point, pretend to be Moe and simply walk away and expect that everything would be fine. Maybe that would be a long-term goal, something to work toward, but right now it was an impossible dream.

Bob stopped, turned around, and went back.

*

Bob hated financial reports. He especially hated reading them. Why? Because the numbers were so depressing. For Bob, reading the reports of his own company's lackluster finances was almost excruciating. The reading was not unlike stepping out of the shower and seeing, but not wanting to see, that his once athletic body had become ponderously overweight. Like, hurry up and towel off before the steam on the mirror evaporates and shows the full truth.

Bob spent only as much time as necessary on finances, because seeing the harsh reality of the numbers was so disillusioning – and because, he reasoned, there were so many other tasks to be accomplished that might have a positive result, even though the positives seldom accumulated. Now Moe wanted an update on the numbers. Bob wondered, could he throw this useless chore to someone else?

He went to Lena.

"Moe has asked for some up-to-date financial statements. Could you please pull them together for me."

"Sorry, but no. Not a good idea in my view," she said. "I mean, if you order me to do the reports, I will. But I'm anything but a wiz on accounting. Plus, I have so much to do, especially now that the HTI order has come through."

Bob nodded and in a grim tone said, "I understand."

Almost from desperation, Bob went to his computer and called up the employee résumés and other records. He began going through them, seeking to find perhaps a hidden gem – say, someone who knew the difference between an asset and a liability.

His search was proving fruitless – until he came to Alice. And lo and behold! Shy little Alice had a degree in accounting! Who knew? If Bob was ever aware of this, he had forgotten. Yet there in her records, tucked away at the bottom, was her graduation from a reputable school granting her a degree in accounting. Good grades, too. Yet all she had ever done, here and previously, was clerical work.

The next morning, Bob went to her and said, "Alice, would you happen to know the difference between an asset and a liability?"

"Well, Mr. Bingham, I think I might. An asset is a resource with economic value that a business entity – a company, a corporation, a partnership, even a sole proprietor – holds with expectation of a future benefit. A liability is something the business owes to another party due to a past event. Examples of assets would include cash, property the business owns, and so on. Examples of liabilities would be, say, a bank loan to the company or the purchase of services for the business that are not as yet paid for. Now, of course, there is also owner's equity – "

"That's fine, Alice," said Bob, sensing that she was just getting warmed up. "I happened to be going through the employee records and I noticed that you have a degree in accounting."

"Yes, I do. Never really done much with it, though."

"Alice, I need your involvement in something very important."

"Important?"

"Yes. I'm not sure you're aware of this, but I have what's known as a silent partner. His name is Maurice Strickett – or 'Moe' as everyone calls him. Moe has the right, according to our partnership agreement, to review the company's finances and to audit them if he so desires. And he is coming here soon to review our current situation. I would like you, Alice, to bring the books up to date and to prepare the financial reports we need for the upcoming meeting. Do you think you can do that?"

"Well, I think so," she said.

"Good! Now, you have to do this confidentially and not talk about our finances with anyone inside or outside the company – with the exceptions of me and Lena. Do you understand?"

"Yes, absolutely," Alice said. "I won't tell a soul."

*

He told Lena of his decision to bring in Alice on the financial reports.

"Do you think she can do it?" Bob asked. "I mean, this is for Moe and if she doesn't do it right, there could be trouble."

"She can probably handle it. That's my bet anyway. She's a bright young woman, just terribly shy."

"Lena, I'm wondering. If she has an accounting degree, why is she content with doing routine clerical work?"

"Alice does not have much self-confidence. She has low self-esteem. She lives with her mother. I don't think she's had romance in her life ever. I've noticed that she tends toward what is safe rather than what is challenging. I'm actually a bit surprised she didn't try to wiggle out of the assignment you gave her. Then again, I think she might be craving more responsibility. There is some quiet war going on inside her and, so far, shyness has won every battle."

"Well, that's more than I wanted to know," said Bob. "We'll see how she does."

"Let me caution you. When she makes a mistake or doesn't do something exactly to your liking, whatever you do, don't yell at her. If you do, she will crumble into a million pieces."

Bob groaned.

"And one more thing," said Lena. "You know Alice's birthday is coming up."

"Really? I was not aware."

"We should get her a birthday cake."

"This is a lot more complicated than I ever expected."

"I'll take care of ordering the cake," said Lena. "A birthday cake will be very meaningful to her. And there will be benefits to all if we start doing more of that kind of thing around here."

*

Bob transferred to Alice everything financial that was current – invoices, receipts, bank deposits, spreadsheets, and so on. After he had done this, he experienced a peculiar feeling. Relief. A weight lifted. And something else: a feeling of freedom.

Since the beginning of the company, Bob had done the bookkeeping for Burbells Universal. He did not want to hire someone to handle this chore. So he did it himself even though he hated it. He would collect and organize the numbers, put them in the journal, and then send them on to the pricey and slow accounting firm for transformation into the required reports for lenders and government authorities. And of course for himself, if he got around to reading them, which he often didn't, because he just didn't want to see how poorly the company was getting along. Besides, he told himself, he just didn't have the time.

Now, it hit him. By taking on – and holding onto – the bookkeeping, like many a small business owner, he had fallen into a trap. A time trap.

This went along with what Moe had said when Bob had been recalibrating the DynaMicro. Bob thought he was saving money and being efficient – when really it was the opposite.

Another time trap. That's what it was.

How many other time traps were there in his life as a business owner?

*

At exactly 10 o'clock on the appointed day, Moe Strickett walked through the entrance to Burbells Universal. Bob had just finished going over the reports that Alice had prepared. All seemed to be in order. After an exchange of insincere pleasantries, Bob handed the printed worksheets to Moe, who donned steel-rimmed glasses and began to read the numbers.

Moe went through everything line by line, saying nothing. Bob took this as a good sign. He was wrong.

"Well, Bob," said Moe when he had finished, "you're not in very good shape, are you."

"Why do you say that?"

"First of all, your cash is not very plentiful. And, related, what is this stupendous number in your accounts receivable? How in the world did it become so colossal?"

"Most of it is due to one customer, High Trajectory Innovations – or HTI. They have not been paying in quite some time."

"A customer is not a customer unless they pay you."

"Nevertheless, Moe, they were our biggest customer. And we have now just picked up an enormous order from HTI."

"HTI ... that rings a bell. Oh, yes, right. The Howitzers. I know of them. Lovely people."

"Are you serious?"

"No, not at all. Anyway, that explains why your materials inventory is so high. You are buying – and paying for – materials to produce product for *them.*"

"Well, yes, we have to in order to build the order," said Bob.

"So your cash is low, your inventory is high, and your receivables are ridiculous."

"Afraid so."

"You are afraid?" Moe asked. "I am terrified."

"I know it's risky business, but I felt I had to take it."

Moe appeared to be on the verge of having a conniption.

"Do you know what you are doing, Bob? You are financing *their* corporate growth, rather than your own. They are using you! Your credit terms are giving them a free ride at your expense!"

"I had to! I mean, what's wrong with offering credit? Everybody does it!"

"Everybody doing it doesn't make it smart."

"What was I to do, sit here and do nothing while someone else walks away with the order?"

"You know what's going to happen? Let me tell you. You have put out your own cash to buy materials, while the Howitzers have paid nothing. And you will receive nothing from them until they have received payment from their customer and the check has cleared. I'll bet you anything that's what happens. Don't you see? There is no risk to them! You have taken all the risk; they have taken none! And if this business goes under, they will not shed a tear. They'll just move on to another supplier."

"What am I to do, Moe? We've already accepted the order. Materials for it are already arriving. Tell me what I should do."

"Either get them to pay fifty percent – you need the cash – or find a way out of this deal."

"But the deal is already underway! I don't think I have the leverage to renege!"

"Then you had better hope that they pay! And in the future," Moe continued, "don't offer credit. You cannot afford to finance another company. If the Howitzers need cash to pay for their own growth, they can go to a bank. *You* are not their bank. *You* should not be paying for what they ought to be paying for."

Moe removed his steely reading glasses, tucked them away in a pocket, and stood up.

"The clock is running, Bob. If you want to hang onto this business – and make it a success – you had better wise up. I already know what I'm going to do. You don't."

"I just need time."

"If you keep screwing up, you're going to run out of time. On the other hand, if you start to turn things around and do the right things right, I'll give you as much time as you need."

Moe stepped toward the door, then turned and said, "I would imagine that your old job at Global Mega is probably seeming to be pretty good in hindsight. A nice steady salary, weekends off, paid vacation ... they might even hire you back. Bob, you can walk away from this at any time. Walk away with nothing, but at least you're out of hell."

He left and closed the office door behind him.

Through gritted teeth, Bob murmured, "I will never give you the satisfaction."

Chapter 9

The Scoreboard

The Easy order turned out to be anything but. Actually, the name "Easy" had nothing to do with difficulty. Easy was the name of the customer – Joe Easy of Easy-Duz-It, Inc. The problem was that Joe Easy, a customer long in good standing, had just placed a substantial order and insisted that he needed it immediately, as in *now*. Bob promised Joe that Burbells Universal would expedite the order and deliver it as soon as possible. Joe accepted this. Bob then went charging out of his office to personally direct the change in priorities.

Since the beginning of the company, Bob had orchestrated the priority of orders, because he alone knew all the customers and which of them truly needed faster delivery. He rarely bothered explaining the reasons for the priorities to other people, because that would take time and, in any case, the priorities were always shifting.

Until now, the Howitzer / HTI order had had top priority, mainly because it was so huge. But as Bob wanted to keep Joe Easy happy, there would have to be adjustments.

"But I thought we were supposed to focus on the Howitzer order," said Lena when Bob told her of the switch.

"Well, overall, the Howitzer order does have priority, but temporarily we're going to put it on the back burner."

"All right," said Lena. "Whatever you say."

However, there were more than two customers to be concerned about. At that moment there were 17 orders in various stages of completion. Some were small while others were much larger – though none of them came close to the Howitzer order.

Bob and Lena went about separately telling people about the switch in priorities. The trouble was that different people heard different things. Some didn't hear anything at all.

What ensued was confusion. And this was not the first time that confusion had reigned.

Bob was walking past Kevin's workstation. He glanced at what Kevin was doing and noticed that he was still working on the Howitzer order.

"Kevin, you're supposed to be working on the Easy order. You know, for the Easy-Duz-It Company."

"I am?"

"Yes!"

"But ... why?"

"Because it's due now!" said Bob.

"Well, how was I supposed to know?"

"Kevin, if you just look around ... "

Bob stopped mid-sentence as he himself looked around only to discover that a number of others were also not working on the Easy order. Some were still working on the Howitzer, while others were working on something entirely different.

"Just switch over to Easy, Kevin."

"But I can't."

"Why not?"

"I don't have materials for Easy. I only have materials for Howitzer."

Bob looked up, skyward, as if seeking divine intervention, but there was none forthcoming.

"All right, keep working on Howitzer," said Bob.

"Are you sure, Mr. Bingham? I could just sit here until the Easy materials arrive."

"No, Kevin, by all means keep going on Howitzer."

Bob then went to Lena to complain.

"You know what the problem is, Lena? I'll tell you what the problem is. The problem is that nobody knows the score!"

"Perhaps that's because there is no scoreboard."

"What? What do you mean?"

"A scoreboard. Something that tells everybody in the same instant where we are in the game."

Bob issued a mild grunting noise, then wandered off to the sanctuary of his office.

*

That night, in bed with Emily sleeping next to him, Bob was thinking about all of this. He grasped that these scheduling and priority changes increased the chaos factor. Added to this were the effects of bad communication. Some time before, he had been walking through the building when he heard two women talking.

"You know," one said to the other, "in this place, if not for miscommunication we would have no communication at all."

Bob was annoyed, but passed them by. Yet the phrase stuck with him. There was a grain of truth to it. Maybe more than a grain.

People often did not understand – or even know about – the priorities. The way the system really worked was based on the information lodged in Bob's head – Bob's and no one else's. So here he was, here *they* were, with two high priority orders and a lot of others as well and it was all descending toward chaos because people didn't know ... well, the score.

"I have to change this," Bob muttered as he lay next to Emily.

"Good. Change all you want," Emily said in a groggy, half-asleep voice. "Just do it quietly when you're next to me."

There is no scoreboard and we need one, thought Bob, *so I will build one.*

*

When morning came, Bob threw himself into creating a scoreboard that everyone could access. In not very much time, just a few days, he had a functioning scoreboard system. There were large-screen monitors positioned so that everyone could read them from their workstations. The large screens made the list of orders easy to read. The order with top priority was naturally at the top of the screen and when that order was filled, the screens would update to the next order. And if there was an update or a change in the schedule, the screen would flash to alert everyone. The system was simply a combination of off-the-shelf software and standard hardware coupled with Bob's ingenuity.

The scoreboard was an instant success. Nobody liked confusion. People instead loved knowing what was going on – loved knowing what the score was. Information is empowering and the scoreboard helped to empower everyone.

A seemingly small detail that became quite important was that Bob himself did not control the scoreboard. Lena did.

This was especially empowering for Lena, but also for Bob.

Within a few days after making the scoreboard operational, Bob experienced something peculiar – but mind-blowing. He realized that he had time on his hands. Every day was no longer a crazy race to keep the work flowing. Bob seemed to have gained time in his work-day, at least half an hour, but perhaps an hour or even longer.

Why? he wondered.

Because, he concluded, with a scoreboard system in place, he did not have to personally intervene as he had for so many years. He didn't have to go around telling people what to work on when priorities changed. He didn't have to run around correcting miscommunication. Because of the scoreboard, people knew what they should be working on and when the work had to be finished. There was no need for Bob to tell them.

With that realization, it was as if clouds had parted in the sky and the sun was shining through. But one realization inspired another.

"If I keep building better systems," he said to himself, "I'll keep gaining time. I'll eliminate the time traps. With more time, I'll be able to take on projects that are more and more valuable to the company – and to me as well."

Yes, the key to it all was in better systems. And Bob was ready to go at it when disaster struck.

Chapter 10

Disaster

The initial batch of Burbells for HTI became ready for shipment, was put on a truck and was delivered. Bob immediately made a "courtesy call" to Henrie Howitzer under the guise of promoting good customer relations, when what he actually wanted to know was when the bill would be paid.

"Bob, I am sure that you will get your money in thirty days – well, sixty days at the latest. So fear not! All is well!" Henrie told him.

"Excuse me? Thirty days? *Sixty* days?! That is seriously at odds with the terms agreed upon! We were expecting payment within *ten* days!"

"Were you? Oh dear. I don't seem to recall," said Henrie.

"Please understand," Bob said, struggling for patience. "You placed a very large order on credit and, frankly, it has put a strain on us. So we would very much appreciate a more timely payment."

"Well, I'll see what we can do, since you did come through for us," said Henrie. "But I can't make any promises."

"Can't make promises? But, Henrie, promises were made! HTI assured us – hello? Hello, Henrie? Are you there?"

She had hung up on him.

So the game began. Each day, Bob would call Henrie trying to re-establish communications, only to have Henrie blow him off with her breezy, casual air. But soon he could not get through to Henrie; he could only reach Henrie's assistant. Then the assistant disappeared. Bob's calls went straight to voicemail, never to be returned.

At the same time, Bob was calling Rupert, the HTI purchasing manager, who once upon a time had assured him that prompt payment would not be a problem. Rupert made reassurances. Then Rupert disappeared. A temporary purchasing manager came into being. She solemnly promised Bob that the payment would be going out "any day now." Then *she* disappeared as well.

And then Moe called Bob.

"Have you heard about the Howitzers?" Moe asked.

"Heard what?"

"There is a rumor that HTI is about to file for bankruptcy, if not today then soon."

Bob's stomach turned over.

"There is a second rumor that the Howitzers have left the country," Moe said.

"But just a few days ago, we delivered ... "

"Yes. My point exactly. Let me ask, Bob. Did you renegotiate the deal as I suggested? Did you get fifty percent of the payment in advance? Did you get the balance upon delivery?"

"No. Sorry. I didn't. On all counts. But, Moe, it just seemed as if everything would work out!"

"Until it didn't."

Bob was silent.

"How much cash do you have?" Moe asked.

"I'm not sure."

"You must always know how much cash you have available. The exact amount is going to change daily. But you must know approximately – if not precisely – how much cash is on hand. And you must also know the near-term upcoming draws against that supply of cash – chief among them payroll, outflows to vendors, utilities, and so on."

"Right, Moe, I've got it."

"Figure out your cash situation – what you've got now, how much is likely to come in, and how much will have to be paid out in the next thirty to sixty days."

"Right. Will do," said Bob.

After collecting himself, Bob went to the edge of his door and called, "Alice! Where's Alice?!"

Lena was nearby. She heard the alarm in Bob's voice when he called out for Alice.

"What's wrong?" Lena asked.

"Oh, nothing much. Just the end of the world."

"What's happening?"

Bob lowered his voice and said, "You cannot repeat this to anyone – although, odds are, they'll find out soon enough."

He told Lena the news.

"How could the Howitzers let such a thing happen?" Lena asked. "They're arrogant and obnoxious, but I expected that they would at least be solvent!"

"Yes, the same here," said Bob. "As I recall, you mentioned that extending additional credit to them sounded like trouble, and you were right. I mean, I feared as much, but decided to go ahead. Yet, looking back and connecting all the dots, I suspect this has been coming on for quite some time. And these past few days, I've had an especially bad feeling. I could sense that something was going on behind the curtain."

"They claimed they had made this enormous sale. Did they really close the sale or was it all made up?"

"I don't know, but there must have been some basis for it. Why would you make up something like that? In any case, I took what I felt was a calculated risk," said Bob. "I knew I was betting the company if things went bad. And they have gone bad indeed."

"What are we going to do?"

"Survive. What's clear to me going forward is that credit can easily become a time bomb. That is something I will never forget. Now, I need to talk to Alice."

He left Lena and began walking toward Alice's tiny closet of an office.

"Yes, Mr. Bingham?"

"Alice, I need to know how much available cash the company has."

"Not a problem," said Alice.

She turned and picked up some sheets of paper.

"Here you are," she said.

"What's this?" Bob asked as he took what she handed to him.

"Our most recent balance sheet. Cash is the first item listed."

"But, Alice, the numbers on the balance sheet are weeks old. I need to know how much cash we have *now*."

"Oh. Well, here is the profit-and-loss statement," she said, giving that to him. "As you can see, the P-and-L shows that the company was recording a small profit at the end of last month. Which I think is encouraging, don't you? So if this month is about the same as last month, we should still be profitable."

"*Was? Was* showing a small profit? That's exactly the problem!" said Bob. "What's on these statements is looking into the past! These do not tell me what the situation is right *now*. What I need to know is how much cash we have *today*."

"Then why don't we go online and bring up our bank accounts on screen. That should give us the current cash balance."

"Right. Of course! Yes, by all means, go ahead, Alice."

Alice logged onto the bank's website and there were the balances on the company's bank accounts. Yet Bob was less than relieved.

"The trouble is that just knowing the balances doesn't tell me enough," he said. "I need to know not just the current cash balances, but the expected draws against the balances for things like payroll and materials and insurance and everything else. I need a report that looks *forward* rather than backward. Something that anticipates upcoming situations – so that we don't unexpectedly hit bottom, like a ship without a navigation chart."

"I'm not sure how to help you, Mr. Bingham, except that many of our expenses come due at fairly regular times during each month. So we could start with those and see how the company's cash stacks up against those more predictable outflows. And payroll is a large expense, but very predictable. Examining those would give you at least partial foresight of what's to come in terms of expenses. As for revenues that would offset the expenses, I'm not sure what to do."

"I might be able to handle that," said Bob. "I know all the customers. I know the ones who pay on time, and the ones who usually pay on time unless they have problems of their own. And I know the ones who are sketchy."

"Like HTI," said Alice.

Bob shot his gaze toward her, causing Alice to blink.

"How did you know?" he asked her.

"I couldn't help but notice while I was working on accounts receivable that High Trajectory Innovations was a bit behind."

"More than 'a bit,' Alice. Now, please don't say anything to anyone, but HTI is the very reason for needing to know how long our cash will last."

By the end of the day, with Alice's help, Bob had determined that Burbells Universal could just barely squeak through the coming weeks. He would have to delay some payments until sales revenues from various customers came in and were deposited in the bank. It was a waiting game that Bob hated to play, but given the bind the company was in, there was no other choice.

*

The next day, Bob got a surprise call from none other than Henrie Howitzer. He of course took the call. The screen on the phone showed Henrie in a bathing suit, palm trees behind her, and there were the splashes and sounds of people frolicking in a nearby swimming pool.

"Hello, Bob!" she said enthusiastically.

"Hello, Henrie. Where are you?"

"Oh, I can't tell you that, Bob. It's a secret! My husband and I are taking a few days off to relax and recharge our batteries. But, as always, there is business to attend to. We're on a sort of working holiday."

"I see. Henrie, I have to ask you a question. There is a rumor going around that HTI is about to declare bankruptcy. Is that true?"

"I would prefer to put it a different way. 'Bankrupt' sounds so harsh, so negative. We're simply exploring our options. But that does bring up my reason for calling. You see, our arrangement with the Big Giant Corporation – how shall I put this? It, you know, fell through. Got cancelled. Complete surprise to us! Turns out they were not as committed to the project as we thought they were."

"Big Giant? That was your client? And the reason for the huge order you gave us?"

"Yes, it was Big Giant," said Henrie. "You didn't know?"

"You never told me! It was yet another secret of yours!"

"Well, in any case, we no longer need the Burbells you delivered. So we want to return them – for a full refund, of course."

"Refund? Henrie, you never paid for them! Why should I give you a refund?!"

"Because we need the cash. Our lawyers don't work for free, you know."

Bob just about had a stroke.

"HENRIE! How can we refund a sale that was never funded by you in the first place?" Bob retorted. "However, we will take the shipment we delivered off your hands – given that HTI defaulted on the terms. I'm going to send a crew of my people to repossess the order.

And if you or anyone at HTI interferes, I'm going to the police to ask that they press criminal charges against you! Not civil, *criminal!* As in go to prison!"

Unflappable Henrie flinched.

"Now, Bob, really? You wouldn't do that. We have such a good relationship."

"No, we do not. And I want you to call your people and instruct them to cooperate with my people when they arrive."

"That won't be necessary."

"Why not?"

"There is nobody in the building. We laid off everyone. Just go around to the back entrance. Enter the code '1-2-3-4' on the security keypad and walk right in. Your precious Burbells should be in plain sight."

And indeed they were.

Chapter 11

A Plethora of Finished Goods Inventory

"Bob," said Lena, "I hate to break the news, but we might have to rent warehouse space in order to have a place to put the Burbells we repossessed from HTI."

"No!" cried Bob. "Aside from the burden on the accounting books, I'm not about to pay rent to house them."

"There is a bit of good news," said Alice.

"How is that?" asked Bob.

"Unsold inventory is considered to be an asset, Mr. Bingham. So that's going to look good on the balance sheet. Or at least it won't look horrible."

"Yes, well, I'd feel better about it if we had some paying customers to take them off our hands," said Bob.

"How are we going to sell five thousand Burbells? How long is it going to take?" asked Lena.

"I have no idea," he said. "That's the problem I'm trying to solve. How I wish we had someone who's really good at sales."

"You could offer a discount," Alice suggested.

"Yes, that's what everybody else does," Lena added.

"In the immortal words of Moe Strickett, 'everybody doing it doesn't make it smart.'"

"Still, the question remains: Where are we going to put all these Burbells?" Lena asked.

"I don't know," said Bob. "Just put them in my office. Leave an aisle so I can get to my desk."

A few hours later, five thousand Burbells were crammed floor to ceiling in Bob's office. He had just enough open space to sidestep to his swivel chair and use the computer on his desk.

*

"Knock, knock," said Moe.

Bob looked up.

"You again, Moe?"

"Yes, me again. I would have actually knocked on your actual door, but it's completely covered with inventory."

"You know, Moe, inventory is an asset, I'm told. So that is to our advantage, isn't it?"

"That's a bit of a stretch, Bob. You see, the problem is that, while it is an asset, it's an illiquid asset. It's money in the deep freeze. You can't spend it, not until the inventory has been sold and converted into cash and the cash is actually in the bank. What you need right now is cash."

"Well, we're going to sell them and then we'll have the cash."

"So are you selling any?"

"Not many."

"Allow me to ask, Bob. Why are you still here? Why haven't you resigned?"

"Because I'm not giving up."

"If I were you, I'd have pulled the plug by now."

"I'm not quitting."

"Do you consider that to be a virtue?"

Bob did not answer.

"Let me ask you this," said Moe. "How is your cash situation? Because cash is going to determine how long you can continue."

"Yes, I'm well aware of that," said Bob "Here ... "

He handed to Moe a spreadsheet showing cash balances for that day and previous days.

"Well," said Moe, "I've seen worse. But the inventory numbers are staggering."

"Listen, Moe, what I really need in order to move this inventory is a good salesperson. Or maybe even a couple of them. You wouldn't happen to know of any, would you?"

"None who are looking for work. Not at present. But I'll keep an eye out for one."

"I'd appreciate it."

"Well, carry on, Bob. Good luck – although you're going to need a lot more than luck to get out of this mess."

"Yes, I know. Moe, you don't have confidence in me, but I swear, I *am* going to turn this business around."

"You? You alone?"

"Well ...*we* – myself and the others working here."

"Ah! Much better!" said Moe. "Teamwork!"

*

As the hour approached five, the employees of Burbells Universal began to put away whatever they had been working on. Soon, they were walking out the door in singles and small groups, going home. They all disappeared – all except Lena and, of course, Bob.

His office door was open and he could see her at her work table puttering with this and that.

"Lena, why aren't you leaving like the rest of them?" he asked.

"I'm staying until I see you leave."

"Why?"

"Bob, you've gone back to working ridiculous hours."

"So? What of it?"

"Let's say, for the sake of argument, that I have a selfish motive. If anything really bad happens to you, I'll probably be out of a job."

Bob chuckled.

"So it's in my own best interest," she said, "to try to persuade you to stop working yourself to death."

"It's a nice thought, but I have so much to do."

"Then come back here after you have dinner with your family," she suggested. "Or, better yet, get a good night's sleep and start again in the morning. You'll be far more productive."

Bob let out a deeper than usual sigh and nodded his acceptance. Still, he counter-puttered to Lena's puttering for a good five minutes before accepting the inevitable – that she was serious.

They walked out together. Bob locked the front entrance.

"See you tomorrow," he told Lena.

"Have a good night."

Bob turned and walked toward his car. Then, after rounding the corner at the end of the block, he stopped. He waited a solid minute, then reversed course and walked back toward Burbells Universal. But as he came around the corner, he saw Lena still standing in front of the entrance, now with her arms crossed.

"I forgot something!" Bob called.

"No, you didn't!" she called back.

"I'll get it in the morning!"

"Good idea! Go home!"

Bob again reversed course, walked to his car, and this time he actually did go home.

*

When Bob entered his house, he startled Emily, who jumped as if he were an intruder.

"You know, Bob, it's a good thing I'm not having an affair, because your appearances have become so unpredictable."

"Ha-ha. As always, it's *so* good to be home."

"You know, I've wondered if you work late because you hate being here. Maybe you hate family life. Maybe you hate me as well?"

"No! That's nonsense. I don't hate you or family or anything. I work long hours because ... well, I have to; there's no other way."

"Why is there no other way?" she asked.

"There just isn't! But it wasn't like that in the beginning. In the beginning, I *planned* to work my butt off."

"Oh, I see. So it was all part of the strategy."

"Yes, Emily, it was! My dream was to work very hard, make Burbells Universal a huge success, then sell the company, retire at a fairly young age, and be completely free. *Free!* I'd be able to do whatever I wanted – and you could as well, Emily. We could travel, lounge by the sea on the Riviera, go on a world cruise, buy a yacht, climb mountains! ... Um, what are you looking at?"

Emily was eyeing Bob's sizeable paunch.

"Yes, I know! I'm out of shape!" he cried. "I'm not climbing any mountains anytime soon. But I'm telling you, that was the *dream*. Work hard for so many years, cross the finish line by selling the company, and then do whatever I – we – wanted to. Maybe start another business. Or not. Play golf. Or do whatever the whim of the moment suggested."

Emily considered this.

"Yes, I remember you saying words to that effect when you were starting out. Seems so long ago. But what happened?"

"What happened?"

"What went wrong?"

Bob thought about this, then said, "I'm not sure anything went 'wrong.' At least, I really don't think that *I* did anything wrong. What is happening now is simply the way things turned out."

"But you had this dream and now ... "

"It's turned into a nightmare."

"How did that happen? Why did it happen?"

Bob sat down at one end of the sofa. Emily sat down at the other. She patiently waited for Bob to ponder her questions.

"I'm an engineer," he said at last. "I'm a very *good* engineer in my own humble opinion."

"Right, I know you are," said Emily.

"As an engineer, I understand Burbells and their incredible potential. And my designs for Burbells are superior. Or *were* superior a few years back. Do you remember when my designs were winning awards?"

"I do remember. I was proud of you. That was before you quit your job at Global Mega Corp. Bob, honestly, were you happy there at Global Mega?"

"I was not happy with what they were paying me, that's for sure. And they never saw the potential, the possibilities, the way I did. Which is why I began thinking about starting my own business. It just seemed natural to me that being good at burbells engineering, I would obviously be good at the burbells *business*."

He was quiet for a moment.

"But that's not the way it turned out," he conceded.

"What are you saying? That you're not good at the business end of things?"

"I wouldn't put it that way. After all, Emily, I've kept Universal going year after year. I'm at least competent. It's just that ... "

"What?"

"Being the owner and manager of a small business is not one job. It's *dozens* of jobs. When I started the business, looking back, I wasn't prepared for all the things that had to be done – that, as it turns out, I would have to do myself."

He looked at her.

"Do you understand? I mean, it's not just engineering and design, which I thought would be my daily focus. It's payroll. It's managing receivables. It's dealing with the late payers. It's cash flow. It's about inventory and having enough of it, but not *too* much. It's about purchasing, dealing with vendors, getting the best prices and service.

It's about hiring the right people and making good choices – and when you make bad choices, it's about firing. Which is a terrible ordeal for everyone, including me.

"You have to know labor law, at least the essentials. And you have to keep pace with the regulations, which the brilliant bureaucrats are always fiddling with. In fact, you have to understand all kinds of business law.

"There is marketing. And sales, which of course is all-important. No sales, no business. And as a small-business owner, I'm handling marketing and sales pretty much all on my own. Quotes to customers, negotiation of terms on large orders, building relationships with our top buyers, resolving problems when they occur – all of that weighs on my shoulders. Actually, not just on my shoulders, but on my back, and on my *head*."

He paused.

"From testing the website and sometimes even answering the phone," Bob continued, "to financial statements and multitudes of tax filings, it's all on me. And you know what? I *hate* it!"

He looked over at his wife.

"Really, Emily, each and every day, I hate most of what I have to do."

Emily, her fingers interlaced on her lap, regarded him with a sympathetic, yet curious expression.

"So, Bob ... "

"Yes?"

"What do you enjoy?"

"What do *I* enjoy?"

"Do you enjoy any of it?"

"Actually, yes, I do enjoy some of it."

"Like what?"

"I enjoy the design aspect. Design is something I'm good at. I love creative engineering. Transforming technology into something fresh. And maybe even new."

"What else?"

"I like interacting with customers – when they're not pissed off at us."

"Anything more?"

"To some extent, the logistical end of things. Especially the problem solving. And I like the feeling of being the owner, of being in charge. At least I used to."

"Just to ask a dumb question," Emily said, "why can't you focus on what you enjoy and what you're really good at – and leave the rest to other people who might be better at those other things than you are?"

Bob rolled his eyes.

"Oh, Emily. No offense, but what you just said is so hopelessly naive."

"Why?"

"There are no other people in the company who are better at those other things than I am!"

"How come they have to be as good as you are? Why can't they just be mediocre yet capable?"

"True, but most of them don't know anything except their narrow little jobs!"

"Well, why can't you teach them to do more?"

He groaned.

"That would take forever, Emily! And I just don't have the time!"

"Bob, if you train them enough so that they are at least competent and can do some of the work you're now doing, you *should* in the long run have more time of your own."

He looked away from her, then said, "Maybe. I don't know. I'll think about it."

"Seems to me that you have to try *something*," his wife said.

"You're right. I need to. The question is *what*?"

Bob turned toward her.

"And speaking of 'what,' but changing the subject," he said, "what's for dinner?"

"Whatever you'd like to make," she said with a smile.

"Such possibilities. How about reservations?"

"Works for me," Emily said.

Chapter 12

Kevin Reads the Manual

The next morning, going to work, Bob thought about his talk with his wife. Perhaps he *should* get others to do more, even if the result wasn't perfect, while he focused on the critical and strategic things that only he could do – and also what he enjoyed and was good at doing.

But as soon as he entered the building, he had to abandon that line of thought. He had a sales presentation to make that morning. The meeting had been scheduled for weeks. And Bob was genuinely excited about it, because he planned to tout the sophisticated custom design capabilities of Burbells Universal. So he did a bit of rehearsing, then grabbed his laptop and squeezed through the aisle to exit.

Almost to the main door, Bob was waylaid by Kevin.

"Excuse me," said Kevin, "but the red light on the DynaMicro is blinking."

Bob looked upwards and exhaled an anguished sigh.

"Are you joking?" Bob asked rhetorically.

"No, I saw it with my own eyes. The red light is definitely blinking."

"Do you know what the blinking red light means?"

"Not really, but ... I'm going to guess ... recalibration is required?"

"Yes, that's what it means," said Bob.

"But I don't know how to do that."

"Kevin, I'm on my way to an important meeting. I do not have time to get involved with this. Can you try to do the recalibration procedure yourself?"

"I suppose I can try, but I'm not sure ... you know, there might be instructions for recalibration on the Internet someplace."

"That's it, Kevin! That's it! Go online. Look for the DynaMicro-512 manual, then do whatever it says!"

"Right!" said Kevin.

Energized, Kevin hurried to the workstation to attempt a solution. Bob went on to his sales meeting.

*

The presentation went well. The potential new customer expressed not only interest but compliments of a technical nature and promised to be in touch if ever they required a customized burbell.

Bob packed up his presentation and headed back. Upon arrival at the company building, he found a fire truck, lights a-flickering, parked in front of the entrance.

"Oh no!" Bob exclaimed. "Now what? *Kevin!*"

He hurried inside. A thin veil of nasty-smelling smoke hung in the air. Firefighters were rolling up their hoses. Bob spotted Lena.

"What happened? Where's Kevin?" he asked. "I know Kevin is involved. Is the DynaMicro destroyed?"

"No. The DynaMicro is all right. It's the Posi-Fuser."

"How in the world did Kevin screw up the Posi-Fuser?"

"He didn't. Not exactly," said Lena. "Kevin went online and read the DynaMicro manual. He did the recalibration, doing exactly what the manual said to do. I was watching him over my shoulder and it seemed as if he did a fine job. However, when the output from the DynaMicro went to the Posi-Fuser, the materials were too thick. The Posi-Fuser overheated and smoke started pouring out."

"Why were the materials too thick?" Bob asked.

Then suddenly the answer popped into his head.

"Aw, no!" he exclaimed.

"What's the matter?"

"I ran into this years ago. The instructions in the manual assume you're using the default settings," said Bob. "But we don't use the default settings – because if we do, the materials come out too thick and the Posi-Fuser overheats!"

"So that bit of information is not in the manual," said Lena.

"Once again, I'm the only one who knows these things! Which is why I have to be here to make sure everything runs the right way!"

"But, Bob, why are you the only person in the building who knows these little details?" she asked.

"Because people don't grasp the importance of the details – or the big picture, for that matter. Years ago, I tried to get them to understand. But people forget! They don't think! They're idiots! ... Um, I don't mean you, Lena – *them*."

"I don't think Kevin was being an idiot. He just didn't know all that he had to know."

Bob sighed.

"Yes, all right," he said, "perhaps Kevin was not being an idiot – in this particular instance. But in general ... "

"Kevin is very upset. He's depressed. He feels foolish. I'm pretty sure he's on the verge of quitting."

"Oh, please – not that. If he quits, I have to replace him. Replace one idiot with another."

Lena stepped closer to him.

"Bob, we've been working together a long time. I'm going to say something that I probably shouldn't. If you want to see an idiot, Bob, look in the mirror. And, you know, perhaps I'm the one who should be quitting."

She started to walk away.

"Wait," said Bob. "Lena, please don't."

"You're a very bright man," she told him, "but you're the one who isn't thinking."

*

The fire truck departed. The smoke was dissipated by way of opened windows and fans. An hour later, Bob and Lena had both calmed down. Lena came in to say that the Posi-Fuser, once cooled, was perfectly functional. No harm done. Lucky lucky.

"I've been considering what happened," Bob told her, "and I have resolved that henceforth I will not call the employees 'idiots' ever again – unless there is a single individual who richly deserves the title, but never as a blanket appellation."

"Oh, Bob! How enlightened of you!"

"Yes, well ... where is Kevin?"

"I sent him home. He was in no condition to be productive."

"I'll talk to him tomorrow."

"If he hasn't quit by then."

"I hope not – seriously, I do," said Bob. "You know he did show initiative, looking up the manual online, then doing the recalibration on his own. Even though it turned out to be wrong, he was trying."

"Maybe you would want to call him today, rather than wait until tomorrow," Lena suggested.

"All right. I'll try to reach him. But, while you're here, there is something else."

"What's that?"

"I'd like to talk about you. Lena, I want to change the way we operate in this company. If the business is to survive, we have to change. And, Lena, I'd like you to play a big part in the coming change. I'd like to expand your responsibilities. How would you feel about that?"

Her response was not what he might have hoped for.

"That depends," she said. "On the one hand, I feel that I could handle greater responsibility. On the other, if you give me more, I'm not sure how that would work out."

"What do you mean?"

"I've known you for a number of years, Bob. I've known you since even before you started the company. I know you have high standards and that you like everything to be done exactly the way that you want things done."

"Yes. You're right. I do."

"Bob, if you expand my responsibilities, but I do something that's not the way that you would do it, then I'm in trouble. I could do things differently, not exactly the way that you would do things, and you could say I was wrong. I don't know, you might even fire me. So, from my point of view, maybe it's better to keep things the way they are."

As she said all this, Bob was frowning.

"Lena, I would never fire you over a simple difference of opinion. And I am serious. We can't continue being the way we are now. We have to change."

"You can try; we can try. But my feeling, Bob, is that you would still want all of us to do everything *your* way."

"Well ... I don't know. Yes. You're right. That is my tendency," he admitted." And what's wrong with that? That said, what I want – what we need – is results. We can't continue if we just stay with the status quo."

"You're involved in just about everything around here, Bob. You want change, but you still want to be in control of everything. And you are personally involved in every function here. If you insist upon doing everything yourself, how can the rest of us grow professionally and improve the business?"

Bob nodded.

"Actually, that is my dilemma," he said. "How can I remove myself from having to manage everything, yet still keep control?"

"I understand," she said, "and I don't really know."

"All right, let me just toss out a question," he said. "Tell me your honest opinion. Let's say I'm not here. Let's say I'm traveling. Let's say I'm in, oh, I don't know – "

"Antarctica," Lena said with a shrug.

"Yes, whatever. Someplace where I can't be easily reached. Let's say that in my absence I've given you total responsibility. How would you manage the business? How would you handle that responsibility?"

Lena looked past Bob's inquisitive, yet stern face. She thought for a moment, then answered.

"Well, before you left for Antarctica, I would want you to tell me everything. Tell me what our goal is. What your vision for the company is. What the near-term and longer-term objectives are. Then let me figure out how to get everything done. And give me the flexibility to adapt. If something isn't working, I need the power to modify it so that it does work."

Bob was slightly frowning as he took in what she was saying.

"Suppose something came up that you didn't know how to handle?" he asked. "What would you do?"

"Then I would send out a dog sled with a message asking for your advice."

He smiled.

"A dog sled?"

"Might be the only way to reach you."

"Getting back to our current situation, if you were in my place as an owner, what would you do to turn around this business?"

"I would give people the latitude to do the right thing."

"And how do you – how do they – know what the 'right thing' is?"

"I'd have to think about it. Maybe we'd all have to think about it."

Chapter 13

A Starr Salesman

A short while later, Moe Strickett called. Bob, already on another call, hastily concluded it and, with a sense of dread, took the call from Moe.

"Yes, partner, what can I do for you?" Bob asked.

"First, you needn't inject any sarcasm."

"I'm not! You're a partner, I'm a partner! What can I do for you?"

"Just wondering how you were coming along. Any problems?"

"No, none," Bob lied. "Everything is good."

"How bad was the fire?"

"Fire? What fire?"

"There was a fire truck in front of your building earlier."

"How do you know that?"

"Bad news travels fast. Just calling to offer my assistance."

"No assistance needed here, Moe. We just had a slight malfunction in a piece of equipment. Everything is back to normal."

"Good. Hate to think of my investment going up in smoke."

"Well, Moe, the smoke has cleared. We're fine."

"I'm fine if you're fine."

"Then I guess we're all fine."

"Excellent. Now, there is another matter," said Moe. "You mentioned something about adding a salesperson to your staff – a move I totally support. It's come onto my radar that there is someone truly pro who has suddenly become available."

"And who might that be?"

"His name is Rico Starr. He worked for me a number of years ago then moved on, and while I cannot recommend him without a few reservations, he's quite good."

"Why is he 'suddenly' available?"

"Until recently, he was working for HTI – you know, the Howitzers."

Bob was looking at the five thousand units of Burbells stacked floor to ceiling all around him.

"Yes," said Bob, "I know the Howitzers."

"Well, you might give Rico a call, see if he's interested."

"And what were you saying about 'a few reservations'?"

"I don't want to taint your objectivity. Why don't you talk to him first and let me know what you think," said Moe. "I'll send his number to you ... "

*

A day later, Rico Starr and Bob Bingham met for coffee. Rico was a tall, devilishly handsome man whose hair was graying at the temples. He was energetic and his attitude seemed exceedingly positive. Bob instantly liked Rico, although there was something about him that made Bob a tad uneasy. Was he too energetic? Too positive? And the fact that Rico's previous job had been with HTI did not help.

Nevertheless, Rico's résumé seemed impressive. So Bob decided to give Rico a try. They quickly came to terms. Rico would receive a small salary, but most of his income would come from commissions that he would earn on every sale he made.

"I have a question, Rico," said Bob. "Was Henry Howitzer as good a salesman as he made himself out to be?"

Rico chuckled and said, "The truth is that, over the past few years, *I* made most of the sales at HTI. Henry was too busy lounging on his yacht."

"And why did HTI go out of business so suddenly?"

"It really wasn't sudden at all," Rico said. "It had been coming on for years. They were up to their ears in debt. The Howitzers had a very expensive lifestyle. They drew a lot of cash out of HTI in order to maintain it. So HTI owed money to banks and other lenders, to vendors, to what seemed like everyone. Yet somehow they were able to keep borrowing."

Bob shook his head and said, "That's a fatal error I hope never to make."

Bob took Rico back to Burbells Universal and gave him a tour. Then Bob mustered the courage to show his office to Rico.

"As you can see," said Bob, "we have a bit of an inventory problem. I'd like you to make this your top priority. Move the goods as fast as you can."

"I'll get right on it," said Rico.

*

Rico started work the very next day. The day after that, 500 of the BU-52 Burbells left Bob's office and were soon on their way out the door to a new customer.

Wow, thought Bob. *This guy moves fast.*

The following day, Rico announced he had just closed a deal for 800 units. Bob watched with a smile on his face as Rico helped John in Shipping pack the order. And just two days later, Rico brought in the biggest sale yet – 1,000 units. Bob could now actually see the floor on one side of his office.

However, anxious to know how much Burbells Universal was making on these large orders, Bob brought up the sales data on his computer, whereupon his eyes became large and wide. Because there was no profit. In fact, Rico had been making these sales at deep discount, bargain prices for the customer.

"Rico!" Bob called out. "We need to talk – immediately!"

"Yes? Is there a problem?"

"Problem? Yes! You've been selling our BU-Fifty-Twos not at a profit, but a loss!" said Bob. "And don't tell me we'll make it back on volume!"

"Well, you told me to move this merchandise as fast as possible! I was just doing what you told me!"

"That's not what I meant. I want you to sell them, but sell them at a profit. And that's what I'll expect going forward."

"That is certainly going to dampen our customers' enthusiasm," said Rico, "and my enthusiasm as well. If I have to sell at list prices, I won't be making nearly as much in commissions. And your inventory is going to be sitting here for months on end. Is that what you want?"

"No, of course not! But I'm not about to just *give away* our products. If we do, we obviously can't stay in business."

"Bob, I need to tell you something and you might not like to hear it."

"Go ahead, tell me."

"Your list prices are high relative to the competition."

"I'm not sure I agree with that," said Bob. "In any case, we're selling a premium product, a product that is second to none!"

"W-e-l-l, that might have been true two years ago. These days, not so much."

Bob folded his arms across his barrel chest.

"You're right. I don't like hearing that."

"Don't misunderstand," said Rico. "This company still has a good reputation, but there are others in the market who are also good and they offer a lower price. Plenty of customers don't need or even want a premium product. They just want something that works and is, well ... cheap."

"I don't think we can do 'cheap' without sacrificing the integrity of our designs," said Bob. "But I do understand what you're saying. All right. Let's see if we can come up with lower prices that are profitable."

*

It was a bit of a struggle to make the numbers come together. But working with Rico, who understood customers and markets, and with Lena, who understood materials purchasing and production, and with Alice, who supplied the accounting data, Bob was able to find and approve a "sweet spot" – a price that was equal to or lower than competitors' prices yet still enabled a profit for Burbells Universal.

Rico resumed selling and demonstrated that he could also be adept at closing sales at a profit. But another issue soon arose.

Bob had adopted the habit of monitoring the entries and balances of the business's bank accounts. He did this daily. Over the course of a few weeks, a mystery developed. For certain, Rico was making sales, but the account balance at the bank was not increasing. Why?

He posed this question to Alice who had a ready reply.

"You see, Mr. Bingham, as soon as the sale has been made, Rico generates an invoice and forwards it to me. I then record the amount and other details in our accounting software – and send the invoice on for payment by the customer. By accounting rules, the revenue shown on the invoice counts as an asset. However, it's not actual, spendable money just yet."

"Excuse me?" Bob asked.

"Well, it's not actually our money because the invoice hasn't been paid. There is a lag. Only when the funds have been received at the bank is the money really ours and, therefore, spendable. This can take weeks or months between the invoice that Mr. Starr generates and the money actually being in the bank. And meanwhile, Mr. Starr expects to be paid his commissions, which is often well in advance of when we, the company, receive payment from the customer."

Bob shook his head in resignation.

"You know, Alice, I sometimes think it's amazing that any small businesses survive. Given the standard backward-looking accounting tools – the journal, the balance sheet, the profit-and-loss statement, the cash flow statement – managing the business feels like trying to steer a car going forward using only the rearview mirror."

He thought for a moment.

"The question," he said, "is what to do about it."

*

What Bob feared the most was that the company would run out of cash and that it would happen without him knowing about it. He worried that dark stars would align and that suddenly the company would not be able to meet payroll (the worst of the potential disasters in Bob's mind) or would not be able to pay vendors, or utilities, or the rent on the building, or everything else. Yes, he could monitor the bank account balances online; that was easy to do. But what if he missed something? The margin of error was narrow enough that just a few unexpected expenses or some invoices that were late in being paid could bring the whole enterprise crashing down – not unlike HTI and the Howitzers, though their catastrophe was brought on by extreme debt mixed with a large dollop of arrogance.

"We need a device, an app, something," Bob said the next day to Alice. "Something to quickly tell us – to assure us – that there will be sufficient cash to cover all obligations for a given period of time – and to let us know after everybody's been paid whether the business will be able to record a profit!"

"I could if you wish prepare cash flow statements – or 'statements of cash flows' as some prefer – on a more timely basis," said Alice. "But the statements would be backward looking, an accounting of what happened, rather than what will or is likely to happen."

"Or, rather, what needs to happen," said Bob.

"Yes. And, in any case, the statements are time-consuming to prepare, especially when using the direct method – which those such as your partner, Mr. Strickett, probably prefers due to the fact that the direct method is easier to evaluate from an investment standpoint. This of course is an alternative to the indirect method, which most titans of commerce and industry prefer. Because it's quicker."

"Alice," Bob said, "you are a godsend. So if I am about to explode, which I believe I am, please do not take it personally in any way. But ... *What I want to know looking forward is whether we have the cash to keep the business going!! Will our payments bounce – or not bounce!? And are we likely to make a profit?? Simplicity! Ease of use! And timeliness! That's all I want!!!*

To Bob's great relief, shy Alice did not flinch.

Indeed, she said, "I'll put my mind to it, Mr. Bingham. Seriously, I will."

Chapter 14

K-Money

Bob went home that evening and chopped vegetables for the family dinner, a quick soup, the broth of which was happily bubbling away on the stove nearby. And while he chopped he thought about everything he had been through with the business in recent times. Emily, who was doing her own share of the chopping, could not help but notice her husband's concentrated silence.

"Penny for your thoughts?" she asked.

"Not sure my thoughts are worth that much."

"All right then ... regardless of cost, what are you thinking about?"

"I'm thinking about the problems and the issues and the continuing craziness of it all – and how I seem to be the lightning rod for all this negative energy. I always hold myself responsible for the screw-ups, small and large, like I'm to blame whenever something goes wrong. Nobody else in the company is like that."

"How do you know?" Emily asked. "People want – people *need* – to be successful in one context or another. If there is a problem, if something keeps going wrong, people know that on some level and their natural response is to fix it so that *they* can be successful."

"Yes. While I am rushing to the rescue in order to be Mr. Fix-It," he said with gloomy enthusiasm.

"Now, Bob, you haven't done it all wrong."

"Haven't done it right either."

"Well, what would it take to do it right? *Who* would it take?"

Bob didn't answer for a moment.

Then he said, "I think it would take everybody. Or nearly so."

"And how can you make that happen? How can you get everybody involved?"

"That's the part I don't know."

*

A day later, Alice hesitantly knocked on Bob's office door. Bob gestured for her to come in and sit down. Thanks to Rico's ongoing salesmanship, there was now room in Bob's office for an extra chair.

"Excuse me, Mr. Bingham, but as promised I've been thinking about cash flow and profit and the difficulties of looking forward so that we know what is ahead of us and we know what to strive for. However, I have a few questions. Might I pose them to you?"

"Yes, of course. Please do go on."

"Thank you. Suppose we consider that there are two general categories of expenses. First are what might be called the 'core expenses.' These are essential obligations that must be paid in order to keep the company in operation. They include payroll, rent and utilities, insurance, routine maintenance, as well as the unexpected."

"The unexpected?"

"As when something breaks and we must pay whatever is demanded in order to get it repaired right away. These unexpected events, whatever they are, should be expected, don't you think, Mr. Bingham?"

"Yes, quite true. Expect the unexpected."

"So there are the core expenses, or outflows necessary to keep the business operational. But there is another category: fulfillment expenses. These expenses have to do with fulfilling the order of whatever the customer is buying. They would include materials, components, packaging, external services for anything not performed here internally, and so on. Fulfillment expenses will float up and down depending upon how much business is flowing through the company, the costliness of the materials we have to purchase, and so on."

"Right. Of course."

"So here is one of my questions," said Alice. "Isn't there usually a down payment the customer pays up front, before we begin to fulfill the order?"

"Yes. Or at least there is now, given what happened with HTI. I mean, sometimes I would waive the down payment to entice the would-be customer into placing the order. But I can't afford to do that anymore."

"Once the down payment has been collected – and deposited in the bank – that money should more or less cover the fulfillment expenses of materials and components we have to buy, as well as services we need to purchase outside the company. Is this correct?"

"Well, we could structure it that way, I think," said Bob.

"So if the money received as a down payment covers materials and services, we need not worry much about those. Where we have to be certain is making sure the margin on each sale contributes sufficiently to covering our core expenses."

"Right, covers what you're calling 'core expenses' *and* generates a profit. Let's not forget about that."

"Of course not, Mr. Bingham."

"Alice, where are you going with this line of reasoning?"

"It occurred to me that if we look at all expenses as mixed together, we will tend to get a distorted picture of what our financial situation really is. That's because fulfillment expenses are so variable. Core expenses are also variable, but are more predictable. Aside from unexpected expense – and we could construct a safety reserve fund likely to cover it – payroll, rent, utilities, and so on are often stable from month to month. This means we'd be looking at our finances through a lens with far less distortion. This means we would have a pretty good idea in advance of the funds necessary to stay solvent."

"Could you give me an example?" asked Bob.

"Well, let's say the figure is fifty thousand in core expenses and profits. That is our 'K' money for a given period, the money we must have to meet our obligations. So long as projected revenue, less fulfillment expenses, is greater than fifty thousand, we're good. If on the other hand we can see that revenue – again, less fulfillment expenses – is going to be only forty thousand, we have to take action, either increase our sales or reduce expenses.

"On the other hand," Alice continued, in her quiet and polite way, "let's say we're ahead in the game and we have a number of times the amount of cash we ordinarily need. Then we can take that superabundant cash – "

"And put it toward an investment that makes additional money for the business."

"Yes, indeed, Mr. Bingham."

Bob sat back and thought for a moment.

"But how do we know we are ahead of the game?" Bob asked. "I mean, how can we be sure?"

"Well, that's the interesting part, in my view. You see, each sale will have what's called a 'contribution margin'."

"What does that mean?"

"Our sales system – its software – will calculate how much an individual order contributes to the profitability of the company – that is, order price minus cost of fulfillment. The difference is the contribution margin. So you would be able to calculate and see early on whether each sale would make money for the company and you would be able to see this in the estimating phase."

"And if we didn't like the margin, if it wasn't enough, we could dismiss the order, right?"

"Yes, exactly!"

"I like it," Bob said. "I like it very much, Alice. It sounds like exactly the cash management tool that we need. Um, what do you call it?"

"K-Money," she said. "Because in algebra, one is always solving for 'K'. So in our case, once we have determined the value of K, we then know our disposition with respect to cash."

"You are brilliant, Alice. I mean that."

"Thank you," she said meekly, starting to blush.

"I'd like to work on this with you and develop a solid system for cash management."

She smiled now.

"That would suit me quite well, Mr. Bingham. Thank you again."

*

Later, toward the end of the day, Bob was talking to Lena.

"I had no idea Alice was so bright," he said.

"For myself, I had a feeling all along that she is very smart, more so than she was comfortable revealing."

"I wonder how many others in this company have untapped potential. Hidden intelligence and talents. Capabilities and capacities that even they themselves don't know they have."

"I am sure there are a few," said Lena. "Perhaps more than a few. But I wouldn't expect miracles."

"By the way, when is Alice's birthday?"

"Next week."

"Have you ordered the cake?"

"Yes, I have," said Lena.

"Good. I'll personally pay for it. And I'll bring the ice cream."

When the day arrived, Alice – while slightly embarrassed initially – sat beaming amidst the attention being paid her. She felt especially honored when Bob Bingham himself offered her the choice of two ice cream flavors – chocolate, vanilla, or both – and served her the first slice.

Chapter 15

Bob's Epiphany

Bob fell in love with K-Money. And as the concept evolved and became more sophisticated, it became more powerful. Bob worked with Alice to keep improving upon her original thinking. He also brought in Lena and Rico Starr, as well as a software consultant to integrate K-Money throughout the company – in payroll, sales, purchasing, everywhere it was appropriate.

For the first time in his years as a small-business owner and manager, Bob became able to track the performance of the company on a daily basis. This was because Bob as well as the employees could see at any time during any day whether they were on track to scoring numbers that would keep the company profitable and growing.

With respect to cash flow, there were patterns. Payroll for example, which happened every two weeks, would significantly draw down available cash until fresh revenue from customers entered the account. And Bob established his own policy that revenues were not to be counted as such until the money was literally in the bank.

Thanks to K-Money, Bob knew how much each sale of a product or service was contributing because it was integrated into the sales quotation system. So he and everybody else could see how every sales quote would affect performance once the sale closed. The system would also provide the accrued amounts for each month.

Yet there was also something deeper happening, something that went beyond K-Money itself. Bob sensed it, but he was unsure of what it was.

Then a piece of what was going on came to him. Basically, he realized that he was having fun. No, not having fun all day every day. But once in a while he found himself actually enjoying what he was doing. That was most unusual.

He was reminded of the early days, before he started the business, when he was designing new products and features and he would get so caught up in the process that he didn't want to stop. In short, it was fun. Now, instead of product design, he was designing –

"Systems!" he exclaimed. "Systems and procedures! Systems and procedures to make the business run better!"

It was as if a brilliant light had shined into his world.

"And if we keep going along these paths," he said to himself, "if *we* keep going, the business ought to get better and better. Which means ... "

He snickered.

" ... it may actually be a lot more fun to be here!"

The very thought of "fun" seemed antithetical to work and business. Bob, however, remembering the good old days early in the industry, recognized that fun and work could co-exist. Not only was it possible, it was highly desirable. He understood this both by memory and intuition.

Essential to it all, he now suddenly understood, was the design of the systems and procedures inside the company. If those were good, he reasoned, then everything became simplified and easier and perhaps even enjoyable – fun by any other name. Bob concluded there and then that systems and procedures were to be his focus, main purpose, and desire henceforth.

*

Moe Strickett somehow noticed something was changing. Whether he just picked up on the vibes at Burbells Universal or he saw some kind of change in the numbers, or some of both, he perceived a swing to the positive. So he dropped by and asked what was going on. Bob told him about K-Money.

"And you've integrated K-Money into Sales?" he asked Bob.

"Yes, we have," said Bob. "Rico Starr now knows what his K-Money targets are each and every day in order for the company to stay on track. In fact, working hand-in-hand with our Scoreboard system, everybody is able to know where we are and where we need to be."

"Impressive," said Moe. "Well done, Bob. Well done. You're one up on me, I have to tell you. In fact, if you don't mind, I'd like to borrow your K-Money concept and adapt it to my other companies."

"That's very flattering," Bob said. "Don't mind a bit."

"Good. You see? Now I'm learning from you!" said Moe. "And to express my gratitude, I'll trade you one tool for another."

"What might that be?"

"The organization chart."

Bob's face dropped.

"You'll pardon me," he said to Moe. "An org chart does not sound ... titillating."

"Do you have an organization chart for this company?"

"Well ... sort of. I threw one together for a bank presentation a while back. But it's very rudimentary. I mean, we're just a small company."

"Yes, you're small now. But in a year or two, you ought to have grown and you might not be so small. Then where will you be?"

"In a better situation, I would hope!"

"I meant in terms of an organization," said Moe. "To expand the business successfully, you're going to have to know which position – with respect to staff – is responsible for exactly what."

"I'd think that would be obvious."

"Seriously, Bob? Now you disappoint me. A business cannot grow from chaos. Everyone you employ must understand what they are responsible for delivering. There must be clearly defined positions with good understanding of how the positions interact with each other and the total process from end to end."

"But how is an organization chart going to accomplish that? An org chart, to my way of thinking, basically says who reports to whom, right?"

"No, that's the standard, static organization chart," said Moe. "What I'm talking about is a chart that is grounded in the present, but can also be easily expanded to accommodate the future."

"That's a lot to digest," said Bob.

"Yes, it is. But in the end, it simplifies a great deal and makes a number of things easier. So, Bob, start thinking about the core functions necessary to fulfill orders. Don't worry so much about who reports to whom in terms of specific individuals; think about the necessary interactions. And we'll go from there at the appropriate time."

*

Bob did think about what Moe had described. To an extent, it helped him better understand some of the problems he had dealt with and was continuing to deal with. For instance, there was the ever-recurring need to recalibrate the DynaMicro. Kevin by now knew how to do the recalibration, but he was the only one aside from Bob. And the process was complicated, requiring technical judgment. Even Kevin didn't always get it right. This meant that Bob from time to time still had to drop everything and step in. Something was wrong in the expectations for that position and the person who filled it.

He remembered the twists and turns of the DynaMicro saga, how he had been doing the recalibration when Moe had come in and been sarcastic and critical. In response, Bob had trained Felix to do what needed to be done, but then Felix had his accident with the bus, putting everything back to square one. So it fell upon Bob once again to get involved – which was when Moe made another annoying suggestion, that everyone be trained to do the required maintenance.

Train everybody? To Bob, this had seemed utterly impractical. But it was worth wondering about. If it could be accomplished, universal training would be the ideal solution. After all, wouldn't it be great to be able simply to assign someone – anyone – who had a bit of time available and say, "Go do it!"

But *how* could it be accomplished. To train everyone in the formal, traditional sense with presentation slides and a workbook and maybe even a certified instructor hired for the occasion would be very expensive both in money and time. Furthermore, in the current situation, with the company still muddling through a lingering cash flow crunch, that kind of training seemed infeasible. They would have to shut down the company for a number of hours, meaning that regular work would be backing up. Then there was the question, what would they really retain? Would every one of them actually be competent in running and maintaining the DynaMicro? How much would they forget as time passed?

The need for practical know-how went well beyond the DynaMicro and the Posi-Fuser and similar machines. There were dozens of processes and procedures throughout the building. Could training extend to all of those as well? No. Far too expensive.

So if classroom-style training was not the way to go, was there another way?

*

One morning soon thereafter, Lena came in. Bob looked up.

"Guess who's back," she said.

"Who?"

"Felix! He just came in. He's still a little banged up, but he's been told he's going to make a complete recovery."

Bob sighed.

"Well, that is very good news," he said. "However, he probably wants his old job back, I would imagine."

"Yes. I think he might."

"Just when we've got Kevin to be competent running the DynaMicro."

"Well, I think above all Felix just wants a job. It could be anything."

"All right," said Bob. "Send him in. I'll talk to him."

Felix, with his wavy red hair, hobbled in on crutches. His broken leg had not yet fully healed.

"How are you feeling?" Bob asked.

"Not bad, considering. The cast on my leg has to stay on another week, but I'm mobile."

"Good. I'm very glad you're on the mend."

"So ... the reason I dropped by is, I was wondering if I might return to work. I have plenty of bills to pay."

"The short answer, Felix, is yes. However, Kevin has moved into your position on the DynaMicro. He's been doing rather well lately, so I don't want to disrupt that. But I'll find a place for you. Let me think ... "

Bob drummed his fingers on his desk blotter while he thought. Then an idea occurred to him.

"Felix, do you remember what I taught you before your accident about recalibrating the DynaMicro?"

"Yes, I think so."

"Then here is what I'd like you to do. I want you to write a manual for the DynaMicro – a manual of our own that expresses how we actually operate the machine in our circumstances, as opposed to the manufacturer's manual which dwells on features we don't even use. And I'd especially like you to focus on the recalibration procedure."

"All right, but what would be the purpose?"

"It's an experiment. I want to see if we can create something that would enable anyone in the company to run and maintain the DynaMicro simply by reading *our* manual. Do you think you can do that?"

"I'll give it a shot," said Felix. "When can I start?"

"Right now," said Bob. "No time like the present!"

Two days later, Felix came back to Bob and handed over a document that was 23 pages long single spaced.

Bob started to read through it, but stopped after page three.

"I'm sorry, Felix. It's clear you made an outstanding effort here, but the plain truth is that nobody is going to read twenty-three pages about a DynaMicro-512."

Felix frowned.

"I gave it everything I had," he said.

"I think that what we want, Felix, is less."

"Well, I could maybe cut a page or two from it."

"No, I believe we need editing that is more radical."

"How radical?"

"It would be wonderful if you could get it down to, say, five pages."

"I don't know," said Felix. "That would mean leaving out a lot."

"Tell you what. We'll hang onto your original draft and if someone wants or needs an in-depth understanding of the DynaMicro, that person can delve into the longer version. But for now, we need something practical, something anybody in the company can digest in a few minutes and then go do the job with no mistakes. That is ideally what I'd like to see."

"It's a tall order," said Felix, "but I'll try."

When he returned to Bob's office, Felix had managed to get the document down to 12 pages.

"That's an improvement," Bob granted after he had read it. "But I'm afraid it's still not as focused and brief as it needs to be."

"I don't know how I can make it any shorter."

Bob thought for a moment.

"Let's try this," he said to Felix. "Let's focus on the recalibration. That's what really screws us up."

"Okay."

"And maybe a different approach would help."

"What do you mean?"

Bob gestured to Felix to lean in closer for confidentiality.

"Felix, let me ask you. Who is the stupidest – no, sorry, that was inappropriate; let me rephrase. Who is the *least smart* person in this building?"

"Well, there are a number of contenders. But if I had to wager a bet on just one, I would say that the person who'd take the prize would be Dizzy Izzy."

"Yes, I think I would concur."

Dizzy Izzy – Isabel – was an older woman, a grandmother, who talked continuously without regard for the fact that much of what she said was a bit loose on logic. Still, she was a diligent worker, always on time, and quite good at repetitive mind-numbing tasks. So Bob had kept her on.

"Here's what I would like you to do, Felix. Write the instructions for recalibrating the DynaMicro as if you were writing them specifically for Dizzy Izzy."

"Okay. I think that's the greatest challenge yet in this assignment. But I'll take a crack at it."

"And one more thing," said Bob.

He reached into the top drawer of this desk, found what he wanted, and handed it to Felix.

"What's this?" asked Felix. "A crayon?"

"Yes, a crayon. I'm thinking maybe, along with the text, you might want to draw some simple illustrations showing what should be done."

"But I'm not an artist."

"Doesn't matter. We won't be sending these to an art gallery," said Bob. "Just draw a simple picture with minimal detail. And make sure, of course, that the picture is accurate."

Felix smiled, left Bob's office with the crayon, and set to the task.

*

And it worked. This time, Felix produced a simple step-by-step document that was something anybody could follow. There were even decision-points – "if ... then" statements – to guide the person doing the recalibration so that the right choice could be made. Later, the instructions would incorporate photos, arrows, sometimes a short and basic video, among other tools to keep it all simple and even obvious as to what the operator should do. And any text was kept minimal.

As the acid test, Bob called upon Dizzy Izzy to perform the next recalibration.

"Oh, I don't think I can do that," she said.

"Just try," said Bob. "Read the instructions and do what they say."

So she did and she finished the recalibration of the DynaMicro in an amount of time somewhat longer than what Bob might have hoped for. But she got it done.

The success thrilled Dizzy Izzy.

"You see!" she crowed. "And they say I'm not smart! Showed them, didn't I!"

Bob too was thrilled. Not only would he be spared the interruption to his own work, but he could already sense the potential of expanding this approach to other machines and processes.

"Just think," he told Lena, "if we can do this throughout the company, we won't have to worry so much if somebody calls off or quits or is promoted to a different position. Somebody else can step in and handle matters."

"You know, there might be something else as well," said Lena. "If we examine each process and procedure while we're breaking it down into its essential steps, we may find ways to eliminate what's unnecessary – and improve the flow."

"Yes!" said Bob. "That's an excellent point!"

So he talked with Felix and awarded him a new job description.

"That's what I want you to do for the immediate future," said Bob. "I'd like you to examine each process and create the shortest, simplest-yet-accurate manual for how to perform that process."

"All right," said Felix. "Very happy to do that."

"Good. And welcome back to Burbells Universal. Glad to have you aboard."

Chapter 16

KPIs for Fun and Profit

Soon thereafter, Bob was talking to Alice when Lena found him.

"Excuse me, Bob, but your favorite business partner is waiting for you in your office."

"What does he want?"

Lena shrugged her shoulders.

"Then I suppose I should go find out," said Bob. "I just love how he wanders in unannounced. No appointment necessary."

When he reached his office, there indeed was Maurice Strickett.

"How's the business doing?" Moe asked.

"We seem to be turning things around."

"*Seem* to be? Are you sure? How do you know?"

"Moe, why are you here?"

"I am here to make my life easier."

"Your life? Easier? And make my life harder?"

"No, not necessarily," said Moe. "In fact, what I am going to strongly suggest will, over time, make your business life easier."

"How so?"

"Bob, do you know what a 'KPI' is?"

"A KPI? Well, it's an acronym that stands for Key Performance, um ... something or other."

"*Indicator.* A Key Performance Indicator."

"Right. We don't use them here."

"Well, I want you to start using them."

"Why? Moe, we have more than enough to deal with here without some 'flavor of the month' management gimmick making things more complicated."

"KPIs are not a gimmick. And they are not intended to complicate anything – just the opposite. They're like gauges on the dashboard of a car. There is the speedometer, the fuel gauge, temperature gauge, and so on. At a glance, the driver can quickly assess what is going on with the car and make adjustments as needed. The same is true with KPIs. They enable you to know how the business is performing so that if something requires an adjustment you can quickly respond."

"Well, I'm all for that, I must admit," said Bob. "What sort of KPIs do you want? And how many?"

"Let's start with two or three, to keep it fairly simple. And I would like you, Bob, to think about what the KPIs should be measuring. What would be the most valuable things to know about the company's performance on a short-term basis? Bear in mind that each of the KPIs should be easy to calculate and easy to update. Once you've figured it out, run it past me. And as you collect the information, I want you to share it with me. That way, I won't have to stop by quite so often. Which is the way I would prefer it."

"Yes, me too," said Bob.

Moe gave him a look.

"Sorry," said Bob. "No offense intended."

"Right."

Then Moe smiled. And it was a warm smile, something as if the sun had just broken through the clouds.

"There's one more thing, Bob. One more thing I'd like you to do. And I want you to do it for yourself, not for me. For yourself and for your wife, Emily. I believe Emily is her name, am I right?"

"Yes. Emily. What about her?"

"This is for you. And for the company," said Moe. "I'd like you to book a two-week trip to someplace you both have always wanted to go."

"Two weeks?"

"Yes, two weeks. Get completely away."

"Get away to where?"

"To anyplace! Go on a cruise! Go explore the meaning and artifacts of some ancient culture! Ride horses on a dude ranch! Whatever floats your boat, Bob – yours and Emily's!"

"But why? Why are you saying this?"

"Listen," said Moe. "Owning and managing a business is both a sprint and a marathon. There is the daily sprint. And you're getting better and better at winning that one, Bob. You're becoming much more efficient and effective as a manager. But there is also the long-term marathon. To win the marathon, you need a finish line. Otherwise, the race never ends. If it never ends, you will burn out, and it might even kill you."

Bob nodded. What Moe was saying was ringing true.

"So this trip a year from now," Moe said, "that's your finish line. That's why you need to book the trip now, a year in advance. Until then, you'll work hard to accomplish everything you need to accomplish. Then you'll go away, relax, revel in your victory, come back, and begin the next race."

"But, Moe, I have no idea what the business situation will be in a year!"

"So figure out what needs to happen in order for you to stand back from the business and go away for two weeks."

"But – !"

"Think about it. Two weeks. Anywhere you want to go."

"I like the idea," Bob admitted. "It would be great to get away from this place."

"To win both the sprint and the marathon, you need not only to race, but to rest. You need balance between your work and life outside of work – family, sports, whatever, fun things you enjoy."

Moe placed a hand on Bob's shoulder.

"You see, despite my criticism, good things are starting to happen. I may complain about this and that, and offer advice – sometimes unwanted, I know. But I really think you're going to win, Bob. I think you're going to cross that finish line, the first of many. You are doing a lot of things right at this point."

Bob nodded slowly and said, "Thank you."

"Now, of course," said Moe, lifting his hand, "you could still turn out to be a colossal screw-up. I'm not ruling that out."

Bob found himself laughing at the insult.

"Neither am I, Moe. Neither am I."

"But I think you'll pull it off. So talk to your wife about where you would like to go."

*

When Bob got home that evening, Emily noticed he was in a curious state of excitement.

"What's got into you?" she asked.

"Nothing," he said reflexively. "Er, actually, that's not true. It is *something*, not nothing."

"What do you mean? What's going on?"

"Moe Strickett came by today and he had a rather unusual recommendation. He told me to book a trip to someplace – anyplace – that we'd like to go, for two weeks."

"You're serious?" asked Emily.

"Yes."

"And you said 'we'? As in the two of us?"

"Yes, I did."

"When?"

"A year from now."

Emily's face, which had been reforming into an expression of delight, now dropped a bit.

"A year from now? Why?"

"Because," said Bob, "if I'm understanding Moe correctly, the trip will be a finish line for me."

"How so?"

"My ability to go away from the company for two weeks without descending into a panic attack will be a goal achieved. I mean, frankly, I couldn't do that right now. But a year from now, the way things are improving at the company, I think that's a reasonable possibility."

In a burst of emotion, Emily charged toward her husband and embraced him.

"That's wonderful!" she exclaimed. "Even if I do have to wait a year, it's still wonderful! You're really changing, Bob!"

Half an hour later, with her head resting on Bob's shoulder, both wrapped in bed sheets, Emily posed a question.

"Where should we go?"

"Oh ... I don't know," Bob said, then with a smile added, "How about Antarctica?"

Emily rose up on an elbow.

"*No!* We are *not* going to Antarctica."

"Why not?" Bob joked. "We can watch penguins frolic. And you would have my undivided attention."

"That would be very nice. But Antarctica would be cold. I want someplace warm."

"How about a cruise?"

"Yes, that's more like it! Or an island someplace in the tropics!"

"So you like this idea of booking a trip?"

"Like it? Bob, I'm ecstatic!"

*

With the exception of Lena Novak, Bob had never trusted anybody in the company. But that was beginning to change. He had gained considerable respect for shy Alice and with that respect came trust. Likewise, Bob's opinion of Felix had risen and he too had become trusted, at least to a degree. Then there was Lena who was always dependable and often insightful as well. So when it came to developing KPIs, as mandated by Moe, Bob decided to include those three – Lena, Alice, and Felix – in the discussion.

He also decided to bring in Rico Starr. Bob did not really trust Rico, but added him to the group because growth in sales was so vital to the future of the company.

Bob took them off-site to a bistro nearby where he had reserved a private room for the meeting. There was tea and coffee, water and soft beverages, pastries and fruit, and Bob encouraged everyone to partake.

"I've done a bit of research about key performance indicators – or KPIs," said Bob, "and I think that once they are in place, they might help us stay focused on critical issues affecting the company and its future. Now, I'd like for all of us to be candid and sincere. So please at any time ask any question you'd like."

"Excuse me," Lena said, pouncing on the opportunity. "Are we as a company growing?"

"W-e-l-l," said Bob, "that's rather hard to say."

"Let me ask something a little different," said Lena. "Are we out of the woods?"

"Out of the woods?"

"Don't mean to be blunt, sorry, but is the company going to survive?"

"Yes!" said Bob. "As of now, I can say that with confidence and with some enthusiasm. Or else I wouldn't be here talking about KPIs!"

"But, getting back to Lena's first question, are we growing?" asked Felix.

"That is difficult to determine until we have more time and data," said Bob. "But it appears we are on the right path."

He could see from their faces that this was not a satisfying answer for them.

"All right, let me briefly tell you the story thus far of Burbells Universal," said Bob. "I founded the company about five years ago. In the early going, sales grew nicely and very quickly, but then more slowly. Growth leveled off. We arrived at a plateau. We've been on that plateau for quite some time now. Then recently came the near disaster with HTI. But that is now largely behind us. Rico has sold off almost all the excess inventory – at a profit in most cases. And we are now, I believe, poised for a rebirth of the company. Which is why we are here today to discuss KPIs – monitoring tools that will tell us if all is well or whether we are slipping into a danger zone. So ... "

Everybody was silent. Bob was having second thoughts about the usefulness of this expedition.

"The question is, what are the three most important things we ought to be monitoring? Any suggestions?" Bob asked.

Still nothing from the group.

"Well, I'll give you one, just to get us rolling – K-Money, which tells us the numbers we need to have in order to meet our current obligations and goals. Alice pioneered the concept and it's a major step forward. So that's one KPI. But we're looking for two more. Any suggestions?"

The silence continued. Nobody wanted to be the first to speak.

"Please," said Bob. "I'm really looking for your help."

Lena relented.

"Okay, just to put something on the table," she said, "how about customer satisfaction?"

Bob winced just a tiny bit, but Lena noticed.

"Is there a problem with customer satisfaction?" she asked.

"It's just that customer satisfaction is so squishy," Bob said.

"Squishy?"

"I mean, how do you measure it in a meaningful way? By the number of warm fuzzy feelings customers say they're having? How do you know if they're being honest or if they're just being nice so as to get rid of the one taking the survey as fast as possible?"

"You wanted a suggestion!" Lena protested.

"Yes, and I appreciate your input, Lena. I really do. Perhaps we could refine your suggestion."

"On-time delivery," said Rico.

"Yes, go on," said Bob.

"I know from experience that if an order is delivered on the date promised to the customer, then the customers are happy. But if the order arrives late, even by just a day or two, then the customers are *not* happy. So if we're delivering on time, as promised, then it's really a gauge of customer satisfaction."

Bob nodded.

"And on-time delivery is easy to record and track over time," said Rico. "Plus, it's not subjective. Either the order was delivered when promised or it wasn't. There is no need to bother the customer with some annoying survey."

"I see. Yes, very good," said Bob.

"You know what else," said Lena. "We could take note of the late deliveries and find out why they were late. Was there a reason? Was it a legitimate 'couldn't be helped' reason or was it that something slipped through the cracks?"

"Right," said Bob. "And then we could work on the causes of the lateness and make improvements."

"Exactly," said Lena.

"Likewise with customer returns," said Felix. "If a customer is returning all or part of an order, something went wrong either on their side or ours. If we can figure out what caused the return, then we might be able to change a thing or two so it doesn't happen again – or doesn't happen as often."

"That's quite good!" said Bob. "Returns cost us quite a bit of money. I hate to say this, but I don't even know exactly how much. I just know that when something comes back, it's not cheap on our side."

"One concern," said Lena.

"Yes?"

"Good luck getting John in Shipping to go along. He gets very sensitive about others meddling in his operation."

"Yes, but John *hates* returns," said Felix. "Anything that reduces returns, John would be all for it – if it's explained to him the right way."

"Yes, excellent point," said Bob.

"One more thought," said Rico. "We could monitor repeat orders. If a customer has a pattern of ordering from us over time and then the pattern stops, then something has happened. The question is, what? Did a competitor offer a lower price? Have their needs changed? Did we do something they didn't like? Or, maybe it's a new customer, but they don't follow up with another order, what's the story? Was it really just a one-time need or did something go wrong? Now, of course we'd have to make polite inquiries, but if those customers do respond with truthful reasons for not continuing with us, that could be ... you know – "

"Fantastic," Bob said.

Whereas at the start Bob had worried that the meeting would be a waste of time, a failure, he now saw this interaction as an unmitigated success. He was getting ideas and insight that he never could have gotten on his own, as a boss.

"All these years," he told Emily over dinner that evening, "I never understood they were capable of such things. And all I had to do was encourage them to think and speak up and get involved. You know, I have to say I love the way things are going with our employees. I love that they're becoming – I think – more like partners in the company. And less like ... you know, servants."

Emily glanced askance at him.

"What's the matter?" Bob asked.

"I'm glad things are changing at work, changing for the better, I hope. Just don't forget people are people."

"Meaning what?"

"People do whatever they perceive will benefit themselves – and not necessarily you or the company."

Bob frowned at first, then grinned.

"You really are a spoiler, Emily."

He sighed.

"I just have to make sure that things work for them," Bob said, "as well as for the company and for me."

Chapter 17

What Kind of Workplace Do You Want?

"Well, that's a reasonably good way to start with KPIs," said Moe.

"How generous of you to say so," said Bob.

They were walking in the neighborhood, as Moe was an advocate of exercise to help keep the mind sharp. Bob had explained the KPIs that had been chosen and, to his surprise, Moe had approved of the choices.

"Over time, you can increase the number of KPIs. Just bear in mind that you need to focus on the most important metrics and try not to focus on everything."

"But isn't 'everything' – every detail – important?" asked Bob.

"Yes, to a degree. But as an owner and manager, you have to keep the big picture *big* and unobscured. You should not be micromanaging every little thing – getting 'down in the weeds' as they say. Remember, to defend everything is to defend nothing."

"Seems to me somebody said that."

"I did," said Moe. "But I adapted it from Frederick the Great."

"Good old Fred. But I stand by my point: details are important. Who looks after the details?"

"Not you."

"Then who?"

"Them," said Moe, gesturing back toward the Burbells Universal building. "Your employees, the people you're paying to get the details right."

"They make mistakes all the time, Moe! Often they don't know that this particular detail should be one way and another detail should be another way!"

"Bob, why have you made it so complicated that they can't figure out the right way to do it?"

"I don't know! It's not like I set out to make things complicated! It's a complex business!"

"Then your people have to know to do what's best."

"What's best? How do they know what's best unless I tell them?"

"Do you recall the day we went to the airport?" Moe asked.

"Of course I do."

"We watched as one of Jimmy Sunn's planes took off. But Jimmy wasn't in the cockpit telling the pilot the right way to fly the plane, was he? Even so, the pilot knew the right way to handle the takeoff."

"Sure," said Bob, "but that pilot probably had thousands of hours of flight time. He was experienced and knew what to do."

"And the employees at Burbells Universal are also experienced, most of them, are they not?"

"Yes, to one degree or another. But I'm telling you, they all make mistakes! I mean, let's be realistic. If I weren't there to keep an eye on things, to catch the mistakes and have them corrected, it would be a disaster! Quality would go to hell. Angry customers would be calling up to complain. And many would be taking their business elsewhere. Why? Because one or more of our fine employees didn't get the details right."

"Let's back up," said Moe. "Tell me something. In an airline company, what are the most important values that everyone needs to observe?"

"Well, um ... safety."

"Right. Go on."

"Courtesy to customers."

"Yes. What else?"

"A tight grip on expenses so as to keep fares competitive and as low as possible while still generating a profit."

"And the values at Burbells Universal?" Moe asked. "What would they be?"

"I don't know. Try to make money and not go bankrupt."

"Rather a low bar, don't you think? Anything else?"

"Never do business with anyone named Howitzer."

Moe sighed in exasperation.

"No, come on, Bob! Let me ask the question this way: what values should you and your company have?"

"Values? Aside from their being legal, I really don't know."

"Tell you what," said Moe, "I'll give you a clue."

"Please!"

"You are a perfectionist, Bob."

"Unfortunately, that's true."

"Why do you say it's unfortunate?"

"Because absolute perfection can never be achieved."

"Ah, but you can still *strive* for perfection, can't you? You might never achieve it, but reaching for it is likely to have positive effects, don't you think?"

"I suppose it might lead to a few improvements. I could see that happening, perhaps. Just one problem, Moe. I might be the perfectionist at the company, but nobody else is."

"Of course not!" said Moe. "That's why you have to draw them into your quest!"

"How?"

"Talk to them! Talk to them often and regularly. Use your own passion for perfection to get them involved. To get them 'engaged' as the currently popular word that is used too frequently. Talk to them, but don't try to feed them bullshit. They will smell it. If they do, you won't be able to get them to believe in anything."

"But what should I tell them?"

"More important than what you tell them is what they tell you. Let them talk and try to understand what they say."

"Oh, my," said Bob.

"What's the matter?"

"This is so different from the way we've done things in the past. From the way *I* have done things."

"Bob, you need your employees to come through for you. For you, for the company, and most importantly for the customers. And, by the way, for themselves."

"Honestly, I'm not sure I can pull this off."

"You've made a number of improvements and that's good. Congratulations. However, you still have a long way to go in order to get the company to run reliably and to grow without your constant physical presence. Don't forget, Bob, that the trip you booked is out there on the horizon."

"That's true," Bob said with a smile. "Emily is very excited."

"What about you?"

"I'm quite excited too!" he said. "We're going to go to – "

"No, no, don't tell me. That's personal and entirely up to you."

"All right. But I'll offer a hint. I'm going to bring you a coconut."

"Just don't throw it at me when I piss you off."

*

When he returned to the building, Bob went to Lena.

"On Monday morning," he said, "I want to hold a company-wide meeting with all the employees."

Lena gave him a quizzical look.

"Yes, I know," said Bob. "I too hope that this company meeting goes better than the last one."

"Should I have an ambulance standing by?"

"That is unfair. No, I don't believe an ambulance will be necessary. At least I hope not."

"How long will the meeting take?" Lena asked.

"Not more than an hour."

"An hour? That's a long time to have the whole company idle."

"All right, half an hour," Bob said. "But if it comes off well, this meeting will ultimately be very productive."

*

Over the weekend, Bob refined his thinking and practiced what he was going to say. He even rehearsed in front of Emily.

"You're taking this very seriously," she commented.

"Yes, I am. All this time, I've been the one who was the perfectionist. But nobody else was. All these years, I was the one who sweated the details. Nobody else did. ... Wait! That's incorrect. Many did care about the details. But they didn't know which of the details were hyper-critical and really mattered – and which of the details merely had to be within normal tolerances. They didn't know because I carried that knowledge around with me and shared only as much as I had to – because I didn't trust them to understand. So I didn't want to waste *my* time explaining it. That has to change."

"Well, I'll tell you this, Bob. You clearly are changing. So it's a pretty good bet that they also will change and adapt and grow. Maybe not all of them, but many or even most."

*

On Monday morning, Bob and Lena directed everyone into Assembly, the only place in the building to have a meeting of this size. Chairs were brought in and were quickly arranged. Most people had seats; some preferred to stand.

Bob stood off to one side. Having thought extensively about the fiasco of the huddle meeting in which he had had his panic attack – disguised as a heart attack – Bob had concluded that the cause of the attack was the result of people surrounding him, setting off a latent claustrophobia that he had only felt a few times previously in his life, combined with a paranoia that people were out to get him. He was determined for this never to occur again. So he stood in a place where no one was behind him.

"Good morning," Bob said. "Today, I'd like for us to begin something new. I'd like for us to work toward creating the kind of workplace – and the kind of company – that we truly want to be a part of. Working here, we are investing many, many hours, days, months, years of our lives in this company. And every company and organization is like that. You trade your time – you trade a large portion of your life – in exchange for a paycheck. For money. Shouldn't that trade be about more than just money? Shouldn't that trade also be about meaning? What does this company stand for? What does your daily contribution to the company stand for? Those are some of the questions before us. What kind of workplace should we create?"

Bob took in the faces in front of him. Some of the workers were intrigued. Some were puzzled. Some were blank – which could mean that they were skeptical or were just plain uninterested. It was hard to discern what was going on in the minds behind the faces.

"So we're going to work on this as a company," Bob continued. "I would very much appreciate your help in establishing a code of company values which guide our everyday decisions and actions. We won't be finished when the meeting concludes today. It's going to take some time. This is going to be an ongoing discussion. Maybe we periodically meet to keep refining the code, adapting it if something is out of date or isn't working or if something better presents itself."

He studied the faces again. A number of expressions suggested that people were confused.

"Are there any questions so far?" Bob asked.

In the back, Dizzy Izzy began waving her hand.

"Yes, Dizz – er, excuse me, Isabel?"

"Pardon me, sir, but I have no idea what you're talking about."

"Yeah, what are we supposed to be doing?" asked another.

"I'm asking you – and everyone – to help me create a code that will guide our everyday decisions. I'm talking about decisions you make while you're on the job."

John from Shipping stood up.

"I don't mean to be rude," John said, "but what's in it for us? For, we, the employees?"

"A lot, I believe," said Bob. "As I just said a moment ago, you're spending a major portion of your life working a job. Wouldn't it be good for that dedication of your time and life to be meaningful in terms of more than just a paycheck?"

"All right, but what do you mean by 'meaningful'?" asked John. "And for that matter, what *is* more meaningful than a paycheck?"

"A lot of things are more meaningful than a paycheck," said Bob. "Or at least *as* meaningful. Money isn't everything, but we all need some."

"Right. But, money aside, what are we supposed to gain with what you're saying? What accrues to us? Like ... ?"

"Like success. Like being a member of a successful team. A successful enterprise. Like being able to go home at night with the knowledge you made a difference. Like being able to quickly figure out what should be done – and without being told what to do."

"I can see all of those as being meaningful," said Lena. "I can see them being satisfying – for all of us, frankly. But it also seems fair to ask, to pick up on what John was saying, yet reverse it, what's in it for the company? What's in it for you?"

"I think that if we establish values and abide by them, the company becomes operationally a lot more efficient. And a lot more responsive. As for me, in all honesty, I think I gain a happier life. Seriously. And I wouldn't doubt that all of you would be happier as well."

Bob again looked into the face of those before him. If he had not reached all of them, he had reached most of them.

"This," he said, "is an adventure upon which we are embarking ... a quest, if you will. Sorry to be romantic, but that's how I see it."

"Mr. Bingham, I believe you've got everyone's attention!" exclaimed Alice – one of the few exclamations of her young life heretofore.

"How and where do we start?" asked Kevin.

"Pardon me again," said Dizzy Izzy, "but I still don't know what you're talking about."

"You'll catch on," Bob assured her.

Chapter 18

A Code of Values

"Bob, you opened the meeting with a reference to a 'code of company values.' What do you mean by that?" Lena asked. "Are you talking about a mission statement?"

"No, not a mission statement."

"What's a mission statement?" John asked.

"A mission statement," said Bob, "is a few high-minded sentences about what purpose the company serves that are chiseled in stone then filed away and ignored unless trotted out for public relations purposes on rare occasions."

"And the code ... ?" asked Lena.

"My thoughts on this are still evolving," said Bob, "but the code, as I think of it, is like a code of honor."

"Code of honor?"

"A code of honor is comprised of strong beliefs that guide behavior. Like, we don't lie, cheat, or steal. We do support and help each other, especially when there are problems that need to be solved. We are polite to each other. We respect each other. We take pride in each others' victories."

"And a company value code?"

"Well, first, a code of honor is a pretty good foundation," said Bob. "But the kind of code I think we'd like to see here is oriented more toward business. Here is one tenet ... perfection."

"Perfection?"

Before him, Bob saw many faces showing confusion and even some fear.

"Good luck with that," someone whispered.

"He's expecting the impossible," muttered someone else.

"All right, I know you're skeptical," said Bob. "But shouldn't we at least try? Shouldn't we strive for perfection?"

"Bob, I think the word 'perfection' might be a bit intimidating, at least for some – and possibly for most," said Lena. "It feels as if you're expecting the impossible."

He thought for a moment.

"Then let's take a verbal step back," Bob said. "How about: we strive for the best possible outcomes in everything we do."

"To me," said Lena, "that sounds and feels better."

"Like we're always trying," said Kevin.

"Yes, best possible outcomes," said Felix. "As for myself, I could get behind that. Because it says 'possible,' which obviously means we're not striving for the *im*possible. We're striving for the best of those possibilities."

"And even when the outcome is actually less than ideal, it still means we're trying to do better," Kevin added.

"Good!" said Bob. "Can we all 'get behind' this idea – to strive for the best possible outcomes?"

There was hesitation on the part of some in the employee's ranks, but most said "yes" or nodded affirmatively.

"Then 'best possible outcomes" shall be the first core value of this company's code," said Bob. "Is there another value worthy of addition to the code? Would anyone care to suggest something?"

Felix spoke up.

"As you know," he said to Bob, "I've been working on documenting all of our processes and equipment so that just about anyone can understand and successfully do whatever task is required. However, what I've seen time and again is needless complexity."

"What do you mean by that?" Lena asked.

"Fifteen steps that could be reduced to, say, five. Options and features that nobody wants. Permissions and sign-offs that really accomplish nothing. That kind of thing."

"But there had to be good reasons for the complexity," said Bob. "I mean, initially at least."

"Perhaps," said Felix. "But when you make something complex, you also tend to make it less efficient and more costly. On the other hand, if you take something complex and simplify it, then you tend to make it more efficient and you at least have the opportunity to make it *less* costly."

"That's an interesting observation," Bob granted. "But what would be the core value that might spring it?"

"Something like, we prefer simplicity over complexity."

"All right, good enough. I can agree with that," said Bob, "although I must admit that I am probably the one who made things complex in the first place!"

A number of people laughed at this.

"So let's include a value regarding the virtue of simplicity," he said. "Now, can we come up with one other value to add to the list, given that three is a nice odd number?"

From the back came a booming voice:

"Service is too small!"

It was Grumpy Gerald with his standard complaint.

"Gerald, this isn't a meeting for voicing complaints," said Bob.

"Why not?"

"Because it isn't!"

"I just want to know when I'm going to get enough space to do my job!"

"Gerald, I believe you have enough space to do your service and repair work," Bob said. "I'll talk to you about it. But right now, that's a separate issue from what we're discussing, which is the core values of the company."

"Shouldn't having enough space to do your job be a value?"

"I don't know. Maybe," said Bob.

"All this other stuff you've been talking about is crap that I don't care about!"

"I will get together with you and hear you out. *Later*. In the meantime, does anyone have any suggestions about meaningful and vital values for the business?"

Jenn, a petite young woman, stood up so that she could be heard.

"I personally believe that openness and honesty are best," she said. "But there are times when some people who have their own agendas conceal things or make shoddy excuses for things that were supposed to happen but didn't. Or for things that did happen but were not supposed to, due to something going wrong."

"What do you think is behind this kind of behavior?" Bob asked.

"Well, it could be any number of things," said Jenn. "Like people trying to avoid blame when something goes wrong. Or, in some cases, people trying to arrange matters for their own convenience."

"She's right," said Nicole, who was next to Jenn. "Things do go on because one person or another wants his or her own way."

"You know," said Felix, "we can be cynical. But some of the missteps we have here are just due to confusion – innocent confusion. The Scoreboard was, in my opinion, a big step in the right direction. But the Scoreboard doesn't always give us all the context and information we need. So in the heat of getting everything done, we don't have access to the information that would help get us to – what did we call it? To the best possible outcomes?"

Bob nodded slowly as he absorbed this.

"He's right," said Rico. "My view, you can't have good outcomes without openness and transparency. You have to be able to see the true situation. And to do that you need transparency."

"Transparency? As opposed to what?" asked Kevin.

"As opposed to having to look into fog and smoke and dark corners trying to see what's really going on," said Alice, who was becoming more outspoken. "With openness and transparency, the fog and the smoke and the darkness is at least minimalized."

"And suppose then that you see things you don't want to see?" asked Felix.

"Then we fix them," said Lena. "We change them to make them conducive to a best-possible outcome."

"That's brilliant," said Bob. "All of it is brilliant – and very true, I think."

*

The very next day, printed posters were glued to the walls throughout Burbells Universal. They proclaimed the core values of the company, as established the day before.

OUR CORE VALUES

1. We strive for the best possible outcomes.

2. We aspire to simplicity.

3. We embrace openness and transparency.

4. A code of honor is the foundation for everything we do.

Chapter 19

Bob Is Serious

Bob was quite proud that the meeting had gone so well and of what they had put together. But there were many on staff, perhaps the majority, who were privately skeptical that the posted values would ever be anything more than mere words on paper. Indeed, there soon occurred a number of tests to Bob's resolve.

There was, for instance, Alice. While she wholeheartedly supported the core value of striving for the best possible outcomes, Alice loved complexity, as it gave her nimble mind a challenge. Whenever one column of numbers would do just fine, Alice was prone to compile six columns of numbers just to showcase the data in exquisite detail.

Meanwhile, as she was preparing those six columns, she would necessarily fall behind on other tasks and demands on her time. So as she overdid one assignment, Alice was often late with others.

This had not escaped Bob's attention. But he was not sure what to do. Alice was extremely bright and extremely valuable, yet she was also still so emotionally fragile that Bob did not know the right words to say to her. So he went to Lena.

"I am serious about the core values," Bob said to her. "I truly am. I don't want to just post them on the wall and then have people forget or ignore what they really mean. And with Alice – one of the best employees we've got – not abiding by one of those values, I can't let that go on, but I don't know what to do."

"Just coach her," Lena said. "*Gently* coach her. She will respond. She respects you, Bob, and she aims to please. I'd even say she wants to please the whole world. But that's Alice. With some others in this company, a less subtle approach would be mandatory. With Alice, you just have to calmly explain the importance of simplicity and I think she will come through."

So Bob did talk to Alice as Lena had suggested. At first, Alice was confused. Why would Bob want less from her rather than more? Soon though, Alice began to see the beauty of simplicity and began to apply it to all of her work. As a result, her assignments were completed when promised – much faster than previously.

Unfortunately, not everyone employed by Burbells Universal was so cooperative. One of those employees was Grumpy Gerald in Service.

Bob had promised to go to Gerald to hear out the man's insistence that his function needed "more space." While Bob did not forget, he had many issues to deal with and so did not get around to it for a day or two. In that time, Bob got a phone call from a customer, Pamela.

"I want to complain," she told Bob.

"All right. What about?"

"We sent a burbell unit for repair and when we didn't hear about the status of the repair for some time, I called to find out what was going on. Well! I got connected to this man named Gerald and he was extremely rude."

"I am very sorry to hear that, Pam. Do you recall what he said?"

"Aside from the obscenities, he kept growling about ... well, something about needing more space."

"I see," said Bob. "Yes, that is absolutely unacceptable. Let us look into it and I assure you that your experience next time will be much more satisfying."

"I'm not sure there will be a 'next time,'" she said.

Bob was just about to go to Gerald and confront him, but paused. On his computer, he called up KPI data on service and repair repeat business. After studying the screen, he noticed a disturbing trend. The number of repeat orders had been declining for some time. Quite disturbing was how few customers did come back for repeat business. There were new service customers, but they generally did not come back after one or two orders. What was going on?

Bob called some of the non-repeating customers to find out why.

"That Gerald of yours made everything more complicated than it needed to be," said one. "Should have been simple, but it wasn't. I decided never again. We won't be back."

"When I asked him to explain what the problem was, he just kept complaining that he didn't have enough space," said another. "I mean, space for what? And why is that my problem when I gave him a problem that should have been fixed, and he didn't do that?"

"He was rude! Why should I have to put up with that?" asked yet another. "He does seem technically competent, but why should I have to put up with rudeness?"

Bob, infuriated at what he was hearing, caught his breath and carefully counted to ten, then went to see Gerald.

Predictably, Gerald said, "I need more space."

"Yes, you've spoken of that before," said Bob. "My question is, *why* do you need more space?"

"So I can lay out all my service jobs at the same time and do everything at once."

"Seriously? Everything at once?"

"That's the way I want to do things."

"Gerald, I would suspect that trying to do all the service jobs at the same time would be tremendously inefficient."

"Nope. Nuh-uh, no. See, if I laid out all the repairs at once, I would have lobotomies of scale."

Bob stared at him for a second.

"Gerald, I think you might mean 'economies of scale'."

"That's not what I said!"

"I know that's not what you said. But ... never mind. Look, everyone acknowledges that technically you are very good. However, when it comes to dealing with other people in this company and also, notably, with customers, there are some serious problems. You not only rub people the wrong way, you can be extremely rude."

"Who said that?"

"A number of the customers who keep the service business here alive! I talked to some of them this morning. And they are not happy."

"Why should I care if they're happy?" Gerald asked.

"Because they're customers! Our business and your paycheck depend on them!"

"But I don't have enough space! Look at John in Shipping! He's got three times the space I've got!"

This comparison seemed odd to Bob.

"Wait a minute, Gerald. Is there some kind of rivalry going on between you and John? Are you *jealous* that Shipping has a larger work area than Service?"

"Whatever! I just need more space!" Gerald cried. "If I had more space, everything would be fine!"

"Let's try something different," said Bob. "Let's look at this in terms of the core values we've established. One of those values is we 'aspire to simplicity'. Now, you want more space so you can lay out all your service jobs at once and work on them simultaneously. Doing that would not be simplicity. Instead, you'd be adding complexity."

"So what? That's the way I want to do it!"

"And our first core value is that 'we strive for the best possible outcomes'. When customers walk away and vow never to do business with us again because of your rudeness, that is not exactly the best possible outcome, is it?"

"I don't know," said Gerald, "works for me."

"Right. And, you know, I'm beginning to think that the real reason you want more space is because you see more work space as giving you higher status, relative to, say, John in Shipping – who, by the way, has many more functions to perform than you do. Furthermore, you have not been up-front about this. When you have secret reasons for doing things, that's not embracing openness and transparency, our third core value."

If Gerald was in any way remorseful about any of this, he was not showing it.

"One more thing," said Bob. "You use profanity without consideration for whether it offends other employees. You're loud. You create disturbances. Those behaviors show disrespect for others and go against this company's code of honor. This cannot continue, Gerald. In fact, I'm afraid I'm going to have to let you go."

"Let me go?" shouted Gerald. "You can't let me go, because I quit!"

With that, he walked out.

*

While Gerald had indeed been a grumpy and difficult employee, he had also been an excellent service technician. His sudden departure caused Bob considerable anxiety. Fortunately, however, Felix had just recently documented the standard operating procedures for the most common service jobs, about 80 percent of the service side of the business. This meant that someone else could step in and perform the service function until a full-fledged replacement for Gerald could be found.

For Bob, the aftermath of the drama with Gerald was a revelation. Gerald had been universally disliked in the company. Bob had put up with his rudeness and his crazy ideas because in Bob's mind, from a purely technical point of view, nobody was better than Gerald and so he would be quite difficult to replace. But now that Gerald had quit, somebody did have to fill the position.

And who might that somebody be? Kevin. Bob was approached by Kevin, who told Bob that he was bored with running the DynaMicro and could he please try his hand at running Service? With trepidation, Bob decided to give Kevin a shot at it.

Kevin did well! By following the standard procedures documented by Felix, it turned out that Kevin could handle the vast majority of service issues. As for the remainder, Bob taught Kevin how to diagnose repair problems – with Felix there documenting the procedures.

*

"I see you've made some personnel changes," Moe said the next time he came by. "How's that organization chart coming along?"

"Um, well ... I can't say it's been a priority," said Bob.

"Ah, but it should be!" Moe insisted.

In actuality, Bob had done almost nothing about the org chart that Moe seemed to value so highly.

"We've had a lot going on here," Bob told him.

"Yes, you have. But the chart is important."

"All right, but why? Why is it so important?"

"For a number of reasons," said Moe. "But first of all, I personally don't think of it as an organization chart per se. I think of it as a 'Now and Future' chart. Or 'NAF'. That's because it specifies what we have now and at the same time makes it much easier to make changes that we will grow into at some point in the future."

"All right. Now and Future. What exactly does it make easier?"

"First, it lays out all the positions and clearly defines them," said Moe. "This makes it easier to prepare procedures – and the process manuals you've been creating, which I commend. As the business expands, the chart makes it much easier to recruit the right people, because you can see what capabilities are required of the person being brought in.

"And because of the chart, people know what their roles are. Responsibilities are clearly defined. When changes are necessary, you change the chart, present it, explain it, get people to buy into it, and then implement it."

"All right. It sounds like it's worth the effort," said Bob.

"Good," said Moe. "Make it happen."

The question for Bob after Moe had departed was, *who* should make it happen? In the past, Bob would have reflexively taken on the task by himself. These days, however, he was trying to be more inclusive, while at the same time limiting his own involvement to the values that only he alone could deliver. So, he wondered, who could take this on?

"Felix," he said after some pondering.

Indeed, Felix was a logical choice. Because of the mini-manuals he'd been writing, Felix already knew the processes throughout the operational end of the company. This gave Felix a big jump on everyone else. When Bob told him that he was being awarded an important new assignment, Felix accepted it with a can-do attitude. Bob watched him leave, Felix walking with only a slight limp.

"Aside from humanitarian concerns," Bob mumbled to himself, "I am damn glad that bus didn't kill Felix."

Whereupon, Bob instantly began thinking about who should be Felix's assistant and back-up.

*

One day, Bob noticed that Rico Starr had a sour and angry expression on his face. He decided he ought to ask Rico what was the matter.

"There is a customer I completely hate," said Rico.

"Who?"

"Maynard Cleon."

"Oh, yes. Maynard. He can be quite difficult."

"He's worse than difficult, in my opinion," said Rico. "I really have tried to deliver a perfect outcome for Maynard's orders. But he's never satisfied. He nitpicks over the most ridiculous things – things over which I have no control. He's insulting. He threatens. And lately he's taken to yelling at me."

"Yelling? At you?"

"Yes. He's extremely disrespectful."

"Well, there is no question that the nasty, arrogant Maynard Cleons of the world are out there. But he *is* a customer."

"Bob, I can't see why being a customer entitles him to harass me," said Rico. "We put in place a code of honor as the foundation for our core values. The code calls for us to be respectful and courteous in our dealings with each other. Isn't it a two-way street?"

"What do you mean?"

"If I have to be respectful to Maynard, doesn't Maynard have to be respectful to me?"

Bob nodded slowly.

"Yes, I see your point," he said to Rico.

"If he can fire us, why can't we fire him?"

"Is that what you want to happen?" asked Bob.

Rico brightened up.

"Actually, yes. I would prefer never to have to deal with him again."

"Let's do this," said Bob. "Let's call him, the two of us, and explain to him that, in the future, if he says anything abusive to you or to any of our employees, then our business relationship is terminated."

"Maynard will not like being given an ultimatum."

"Well, probably not. But at least we will have offered an opportunity for him to mend his ways."

So they called and not even a minute into the call Maynard broke into a horrendous diatribe with highly insulting language.

"That's *it*, Mr. Cleon," said Bob. "We are through. We will deliver any orders you've placed with us that are currently unfilled. And then we will have nothing further to do with you. Good-bye."

As soon as the call ended, Rico Starr was beaming with both relief and pride.

"Bob, thank you for backing me up," he said. "I really appreciate it. And I promise you I will gain back the business that was lost by standing up to Maynard Cleon. Thank you again."

Rico did set himself tirelessly to the task and within a week he had closed a sale with a new customer that more than made up for Cleon's lost business – and the new customer was even pleasant to work with.

*

News of how Bob had risen to Rico's defense and given the boot to an abusive customer caused a quiet sensation throughout Burbells Universal. And this had come on the heels of Grumpy Gerald's departure. Both situations were rectified through the application of the company's code of honor and its core values. The conclusion being drawn was that the company was not *all* about money. Not *all* about profit. Not even *all* about practicality. There were now principles involved. Decisions were being made and actions were being taken based on stated values embodied in a code. That was viewed by anyone who thought about it as a very positive development.

"I do believe Mr. Bingham is serious," Alice confided to Lena. "The values are more than just wishful thinking."

"Yes, I agree," said Lena. "He's taking it all seriously. And, because of that, so am I."

Alice reflected on this for a few seconds.

"I think most people would like to see this work," she said. "So they're getting on board. And so I have to say that I am on board myself."

Chapter 20

Fuggy

Moe dropped by unannounced one morning. He had not done this in some time. Nevertheless, Bob was not exactly thrilled to see him.

"Well, hello, fellow investor," he said to Moe. "What compelled you to wander in? A chance to say 'thank you' for our fine performance in the marketplace?"

"I've noticed a decline in one of your key performance indicators," said Moe. "Do you know what I'm referring to?"

"The percentage of on-time deliveries has dropped – not by much, but it has come down."

"Why do you think that's happened?"

"Offhand, I'm not entirely sure. Maybe just normal variation," said Bob. "But let's not forget the good news. Our sales are up! Rico Starr is doing a tremendous job. Sales revenues are up twenty percent over this time last year."

"Do you think there could be a relationship between the two? Between an increase in sales and a decline in on-time deliveries?"

"I'm not sure what you're getting at."

"Have you added any new employees or equipment to help keep up with rising demand?" asked Moe.

"Um, no, I haven't. I just assumed that some extra effort on the part of everybody currently on the payroll would get us through."

"But the decline in on-time deliveries should tell you that 'extra effort' – overtime – is not going to carry the day. It's a temporary solution, not a permanent one. If sales continue to increase, you're going to experience constraints that limit the flow through the business system."

"You're talking about bottlenecks?" asked Bob.

"Yes, but they are occurring because of rising sales – rising demand for your burbells. You had no bottlenecks prior to the increase in sales because demand was low. But as sales increase that can change."

"Sorry, not sure I understand."

"Every resource – people, equipment, and so on – has limited, not infinite capacity. So as the market pulls more and more product through your system, you're eventually going to hit the limit of at least one resource. Whatever that resource happens to be will become the constraint on the total system. And I think that is what's happening now. Do you follow me?"

"Yes. Or I think so."

"Now while we're on the subject, you mentioned bottlenecks."

"Right."

"What does an actual bottleneck on, say, a wine bottle do?"

Bob shrugged.

"The neck of the bottle regulates the flow," said Moe. "That's its purpose; that's why it is there. Without the bottleneck, you would have difficulty managing the flow – and you could end up with an awful mess. Which is also what happens in a lot of businesses. They eliminate the bottleneck rather than managing it. And they often end up with an awful mess – with a business system that is very sloppy and hard to control. A good, proper bottleneck is a useful thing. You just have to know where it is and what it is."

"How do I find it?" asked Bob.

"It's not terribly difficult. Look at where the flow through the system is slowing down, where it's backing up, where work-in-process has to wait rather than be processed immediately. But remember, as long as the bottleneck – the 'system constraint' as it's often called – as long as it's at least equal to market demand, you're fine. As long as you manage it well, the system constraint is your friend, not your enemy."

Bob stroked his chin, unsure of what to make of all this.

"However," Moe continued, "given that on-time deliveries have fallen, I'd say you probably need to add some capacity to wherever the bottleneck is. The easiest thing to do is to hire more people – one or two, in your case, not dozens. And you should start now, because good people can be hard to find."

"Yes, I'll get right on it," said Bob.

*

As Moe had predicted, the bottleneck was not hard to find. Some people already knew where it was. Though they might not have called it a bottleneck, it was just always falling behind. Lena in particular knew, but she had done nothing about it one way or the other, because she still depended upon Bob to tell her what needed to be done and to approve her every action. Bob identified it by walking around and carefully observing where production flow was slowing down and backing up – then double-checking it by examining the numbers.

The bottleneck occurred at the HyperSpinner. There was visual evidence. Next to the HyperSpinner was a huge stack of work-in-process inventory – or WIP – sitting there waiting. And it was far more than the WIP at other processes along the way. Furthermore, the operator, whose name was Nathan, was logging a lot of overtime in order to keep up with demand. Bob talked to him.

"Nathan, why do you think the flow bogs down here at HyperSpinning?"

"Well, it's a time-consuming process, more so than the other steps along the way. But the other thing is the preparation that has to be done before the spinning can begin. And I've only got two hands, you know."

"So if I got you someone to do some or all of the prep work, would that help?"

"Yes, I'm sure it would," said Nathan.

"Would you happen to know someone who might be qualified?"

"There's my brother-in-law. I think he's done spinning in the past. At least that's what he tells me."

"What's his name?"

"Hugh Fuggelston – but everyone calls him Fuggy. Here, let me give you his number."

Bob called Fuggy and met with him. Anxious to solve the problem quickly, Bob hired him on the spot and put him to work the next day. He walked Fuggy through the core values, giving each a brief explanation, and showed Fuggy the instructions Felix had prepared on HyperSpinning preparation. Fuggy listened agreeably and when prompted told Bob that he understood everything.

"Good, that should take care of that," Bob told himself. "Problem solved."

*

But it was soon revealed that hiring Fuggy did not take care of anything. In fact, he made things worse. Despite claiming that he understood how to do the prep, he couldn't seem to get the hang of it. So Nathan had to interrupt what he was doing to give Fuggy some pointers. As days passed, Fuggy became almost competent – as long as he paid attention to what he was doing.

Fuggy had two speeds: "too fast" and "stopped". He would rush through a batch of the prep work, a man in constant motion, blazing away, giving every appearance of being a production superhero. And then when the batch was prepped, Fuggy would disappear. He always claimed to be on break, but the breaks became longer and longer. He was very good at hiding. He would be around the corner playing games on his phone. Or he would be chatting with one or more of the younger female employees, distracting them from the work they were supposed to be doing.

An even bigger problem, however, was that most of his output was slapdash. His work was at best barely acceptable, but was just plain sloppy and sometimes inadequate. When Nathan, who was conscientious, spotted a piece that just would not do, he would break off from his HyperSpinning to fix or finish what Fuggy had neglected before he went "on break". So Nathan was effectively doing everything – essentially doing two jobs rather than focusing on one – and all the while output from the HyperSpinner was not improving. And there was the added burden of Fuggy's wages and benefits weighing on productivity.

Nathan of course resented this. But in order to protect his brother-in-law – actually, to protect his long-suffering sister – he said nothing to anyone, although he did exchange words with Fuggy in angry yet hushed tones.

However, Fuggy's anti-productive behaviors did not go unnoticed. Lena came around a corner into a seldom used and dimly lit part of the building. And there was Fuggy leaning against the wall, his face illuminated by the light of the screen on his phone. He startled Lena.

"What are you doing here?" she asked.

"Nothing."

"I can see that."

"Just taking a break."

"Yes, well, we have several top priority orders we need to produce and ship as soon as we can. I think you should be helping Nathan, which is why you're being paid."

"Right. Be there in a few."

Lena went on, but noted the time. She also noted a short while later that it took Fuggy fifteen minutes to return to his station. More than "a few". From that point on, she never trusted him.

In the meantime, ever since hiring Fuggy, Bob had been monitoring the metrics and looking for improvement. But there was no improvement. On-time deliveries were still in decline. He went to Lena.

"What's going on?" he asked her. "I hired a helper for Nathan, but the situation is not improving."

"It's the new guy, Fuggy. He's useless. In fact, he's worse than useless."

She told him everything she knew. Bob shut his eyes due to the mental pain caused by the magnitude of his mistake.

"Well, sounds like I made a mistake," he said. "What's to be done about it in your opinion?"

"Not my call, Bob."

"Why? You are the company's operations manager."

"In theory."

"What do you mean by that?" Bob asked. "Wait. Never mind. We'll come back to that another time. Right now, we've got to deal with Fuggy. So let me ask you this, Lena. Is he salvageable?"

"No."

"I mean, if we were patient and gave him another chance, you know, to embrace the company's core values – "

"Fuggy is a colossal screw-up. He's not trustworthy. He's careless. And the only thing Fuggy embraces is himself."

"So if I were not here and you had to make the decision, you would let him go?"

"Immediately if not sooner."

*

Bob wasn't looking forward to confronting Fuggy. Bob remembered something Moe had said when they had discussed company values – "You know, Bob, if you have these values in place it makes it much easier to explain to someone why you're letting them go. Except for sadists, most managers dread that task, it's emotionally wrenching for both the people involved. But sometimes it's necessary." Bob looked back at how Gerald had made it easy by quitting anyway, and had prepared for Fuggy by identifying the values Fuggy had disregarded.

However, Fuggy made it easy for Bob. As Bob was explaining the reasons for termination, Fuggy actually yawned. He just didn't care. Not many minutes later, Fuggy was out the door.

Chapter 21

What Goes Wrong Can Be Made Right

After the Fuggy fiasco, Bob became retrospective.

"What went wrong?" he wondered aloud to Lena. "Why in the world did I ever hire him?"

"Wait. Back up, Bob. What exactly happened?"

"I – or we – determined that the HyperSpinner had become a bottleneck due to increasing sales and the inability of the spinning process to keep up with demand. So I asked Nathan if hiring a helper to do the prep work would be beneficial. Nathan said yes."

"And?"

"And Nathan recommended his brother-in-law."

"Maybe that was the first mistake?"

"Was it a mistake? Nathan is a good worker, so I presumed that anyone Nathan recommended would be like him. Or have values like his – values like ours. I think *that* was the mistake, or the beginning of the mistake. Being Nathan's brother-in-law is kind of irrelevant, because Fuggy – if he had the right values – could have turned out to be competent and conscientious. But when I was interviewing him, I didn't find out who Fuggy really was."

"Why is that, do you think?"

"Because I was in a hurry," said Bob. "We've got customers waiting. I've got Moe Strickett breathing down my neck, all bothered about the drop in on-time deliveries. Which is appropriate; I'm bothered too. So in a rush, I hired Fuggy, taking him at face value."

"There was a lot of deception on his part," said Lena.

"Yes, there was. He was acting. Goes on all the time I suspect. Not just with him. You have an open position, people apply for it, and the unscrupulous ones tell you whatever they think you want to hear in order to get the job. I should have known better, Lena. I should have looked into Fuggy's past. Into his character. And until I had a better sense of who he was, I shouldn't have hired him. Of course, if I had known his true character, I wouldn't have hired him at all!"

"Well, that's all water over the dam ... or under the bridge, whichever you prefer," said Lena.

"The question is, what should be done now? Nathan still needs a helper because we need him to focus on spinning and relieve him of the prep work. But how long will it take to find and hire the right helper? What I've learned is not to be hasty in hiring. Yet we need someone *now*."

*

Fortunately, a solution – at least a temporary one – presented itself that same day. Lena was on her way to speak with John in Shipping about an issue that had come up. She came upon an employee named Marie who was just standing there doing absolutely nothing.

"Excuse me," said Lena, "but why aren't you working?"

"Because I have nothing to work on," Marie said. "I finished the last of it an hour ago."

"Really?"

"Yes. I'm told everything is being held up at the spinner. So I'm waiting. And I hate it! Time goes so slowly when there is nothing to do. I'd much prefer to be busy doing something useful."

"All right then," said Lena. "Please come with me."

She took Marie through the building, over to the HyperSpinner where Nathan was frantically doing the prep work left unfinished by Fuggy.

"Nathan, do you know Marie? She's going to be your helper – at least for today."

"Good enough," said Nathan. "I'll be very happy to have the help."

"She can look at the procedure that Felix drew up, but you may have to coach her a bit as well."

"Not a problem," said Nathan.

Later, Lena went to Bob and explained what she had done.

"That's excellent," said Bob. "Why didn't I think of that?"

"You have plenty to think about."

"Well, I'm glad you had the presence of mind to do something."

"The point is that there will be slack in the workflow. Hardly anybody is or can be one hundred percent busy all the time. So move those with slack time to places where they can be productive and improve the flow. This Marie is a treasure! She actually *wants* to work rather than do nothing and get paid."

"Yes, that's very good, Lena. But I have a question for you. As sales were rising, the bottleneck was developing and on-time deliveries were suffering. You knew this, didn't you? Why didn't you take action and do something?"

Embarrassed, Lena looked toward the floor.

"Honestly, Bob, I was waiting for you. I was waiting for you to say something. Old habits are hard to break."

"True – and I am not one to talk. But for the record, as long as your actions are in line with the core values, I will never hold it against you, even if your actions turn out to be misguided. If you see an opportunity – like today with Marie – or a problem developing, you don't have to wait for my approval. Take action – action that is responsible and in line with our values. No longer, I swear, do you have to wait for me."

"All right," said Lena. "It's a deal."

*

Yet the kind of improvising that Lena did to take advantage of a bit of idle time on the part of Marie or another worker was not really a complete solution. There were often times when nobody was idle. And there were employees who were not as flexible or as willing as Marie. The permanent solution was to hire someone new – but to do the selection and hiring in a way that would avoid another Fuggleston flop.

They sent out video and text advertisements soliciting people to apply for the position. And they got a number of replies. Some could be immediately discarded. Others, however, showed potential in the applicants.

One of them was Corey Maxwell, a younger man with a technical degree from a local school. Bob was not overly impressed when he first met Corey. But Corey kept showing up on time and suitably attired for the job interviews, of which there were several. Others did not show up.

The multiple interviews were with not only Bob, but also Lena, as well as Nathan and also with Marie. Nathan was a natural choice because the applicant selected would be working with him. Marie was invited to sit in, because she personified many of the values they were seeking in an employee.

The process took time, all the more so because they were evaluating three other candidates. But in the end, they concluded that Corey had long-term potential. He was bright, had a strong work ethic, was honest in what he said, picked up on things quickly, and he was interested in not only the HyperSpinner, but the whole operation.

"I can see him becoming a really good team leader someday," Lena commented.

"Yes, he can definitely become more than a helper," Bob said.

As a final step, almost like insurance in case they had missed something, they offered Corey temporary employment – paid of course – and he began working with Nathan. After a relatively short time, though, it was clear that Corey was a winner. Bob offered to make his position permanent and Corey accepted.

"Thank you," Corey said sincerely. "Thank you so much. I really need this job. I appreciate it."

*

With Corey doing the prep work, the bottleneck at the HyperSpinner was eliminated. Flow through that station increased.

After a couple of weeks Bob and Lena were alarmed that the number of on-time deliveries hadn't improved by very much.

Lena investigated, and quickly identified the issue. She went to see Bob.

"Bob," she began, "the good news is that we cleared the HyperSpinner bottleneck. The bad news is that it's shown up a lack of capacity in Packaging. They can't cope with the increased workflow."

"Oh," said Bob, "I guess we should have foreseen that possibility! What should we do? Any ideas Lena?"

"Well, they're working flat out, and I can't think of any automation that could help. We need another pair of hands. In the meantime we can pay some overtime and draft in some help from other processes where there's a bit of slack."

So they went again into hiring mode.

But Bob was worried – so worried that he picked up his phone and called Moe Strickett.

*

"You're becoming a man of surprises," Moe told him.

"How so?"

"Instead of waiting for me to drop in, you're actually calling *me*. What's the problem?"

"Well, as you know," said Bob, "sales had increased to the extent that the HyperSpinner became a bottleneck limiting the flow of what we could ship and deliver on time. After a terrible mistake, we hired the right person in the end and he's working out quite well. Capacity on the Spinner has increased as a result and flow through that process is now more than adequate."

"However?"

"The bottleneck has moved. Or perhaps a better way to say it is that a new bottleneck has been created – unintentionally of course. My question, Moe, is whether this is going to keep happening? Is fulfillment going to go down every time sales go up?"

"That doesn't have to be the case," said Moe. "And naturally you don't want it to be the case."

"Then how do I prevent these wandering bottlenecks from occurring?"

"You have to analyze the complete beginning to end system and calculate what it's really capable of. And then you have to have Rico Starr put together a sales forecast. Then you compare the two and estimate whether the capacity of the *slowest* process will be equal to or greater than demand. You also want to examine problem-prone procedures that will likely cause delays if they break down. That will give you and your people some idea of where potential bottlenecks could appear. That way you can add reserve capacity or at least be prepared for what might occur."

"Sounds reasonable," said Bob.

"But there is something else to think about. Do you remember when I talked about having a system constraint?"

"Yes, I do."

"A system constraint is something that regulates the flow of whatever you're creating. Think of a system constraint as being like a valve, rather than something with a fixed capacity like a bottleneck."

"So a system constraint and a bottleneck are different?"

"Yes. A true bottleneck, as I think of it, is some finite resource that you have to live with – not much you can do about it, except manage it as intelligently as you can. What you are experiencing, Bob, are temporary bottlenecks caused by – of all things – success. You can and probably should eliminate them as soon as you can, especially if demand is going to keep rising. But a system constraint is something you deliberately put in place and preserve."

"Now why would I want to do that?" Bob asked.

"Workflow management. And speed."

"Sorry, I don't understand."

"Let's say your car has, oh, three hundred horsepower. That is, the engine can develop three hundred horsepower if it's needed. Most of the time, though, you don't need three hundred horsepower. So you're using a fraction of the engine's total capacity in normal driving. But there are going to be times when you need to go faster. That's when that extra horsepower becomes very useful – even necessary."

"All right, but I don't see what that has to do with the on-time delivery of Burbells."

"Speed. You need the speed for generating superior performance, but also to recover from negative variation."

"Meaning ... ?"

"There will always be variability – both positive and negative. On the positive side, sometimes things go swimmingly well and you're ahead in the game. On the negative side, you can fall behind due to slowdowns, breakdowns, a shortage of materials, late deliveries from one of your suppliers, sudden shit showers. And you must be able to recover from these as soon as possible. Hence, speed."

"Of course."

"Now there are some who suggest that extra capacity is the equivalent of *excess* capacity. And that excess capacity is a form of waste. Well, in the extreme, perhaps. But generally you need extra capacity – not excess, but extra, as above the norm yet available when needed."

"You spoke of a system constraint. What does it do?"

"It prevents chaos. And it increases predictability. With a system constraint, the rate of flow through the system is equal to the rate at which you can ship and deliver. That's provided that nothing on either side of the constraint disrupts the flow."

"So dependability, reliability ... these would come into play."

"Yes, exactly, Bob. Reliability, process control, quality – all of these are woven together."

"But, Moe, are you actually suggesting that we *establish* a constraint?"

"A system constraint. Yes."

"Establish it where?"

"Wherever it gives you the most systemic control. Just remember you want it to behave like a valve, not a bottleneck."

"A valve ... ?"

"Yes. As demand rises, you want the ability to increase the volume. A valve allows this. Conversely, if demand falls – as in a recession – you want the ability to reduce the volume without losing speed and flow."

"Well, where would you put the constraint?"

"One of the better places to put the system constraint is at the beginning, with the release of materials for processing. You only allow into the system what demand calls for. But if you cannot place the constraint at the beginning, that's fine too. If the constraint is in the middle of operations or even at the end, you set up communication so that the constraint triggers the release of more materials when needed. Just choose a resource that is reliable and easily observable."

"But what about everything else?"

"Everything else serves the needs of the system constraint."

"How do you synchronize everything overall?

"I hear what you're saying, Bob. And it's the micro-manager in you that's speaking. Think of it this way: rather than trying to micromanage everything, what has to be done is to micromanage the system constraint. Everything else pretty much falls into place. I think even you could handle that, Bob."

"Moe, you have such a way of being supportive yet insulting."

"Thank you, Bob. Appreciate it."

"All right, kidding aside, there is a favor I would ask of you."

"What's that?"

"Would you – and I can't believe I'm saying this – would you please come by again soon and explain all this about system constraints and so on to me and my staff?"

"Yes, certainly – especially if it may increase the likelihood at last of a return on my investment."

Chapter 22

Simplicity

Soon thereafter, an amazing realization came to Bob. The time of day was late in the afternoon. Bob looked up after finishing a task and it occurred to him that there was nothing else he had to do. He could go home early. When was the last time that had happened? Not since before he had started the business.

He was just about to do that when his phone rang. The caller was Ned Meyers, a client whose enthusiasm for custom-designed Burbells was exceeded by none – although Bob's own penchant for customized designs had once been something they had shared. But not so much these days, however.

"So how is the new design for me coming along?" Ned asked.

"Um, it's coming," Bob replied.

In truth, he had all but forgotten about it given everything else that was going on. At this point, Ned's advanced custom design was more than a month behind schedule.

"Glad to hear it's on its way," said Ned. "But when can I see something?"

"I think I can have it to you tomorrow," Bob said while hoping he wasn't overpromising.

"Excellent! Give me a call as soon as it's finished so I can make time to review it with you."

"Will do," said Bob.

And so there went Bob's opportunity to leave early. He went immediately to Service, brought up the design for Ned on the workstation screen, and went at it.

The next thing he knew, the time was seven o'clock and his phone was again ringing. His wife was calling.

"Should I save dinner for you or are you on your way?" Emily asked in a chilly tone.

"Oh, nuts," said Bob. "I'm sorry, dear. I got caught up in a design and I lost all track of the time. I'll be leaving in a few minutes."

"You're serious? You're not going back to the ways of the old Bob Bingham, are you?"

Now Bob was irritated.

"No, Emily, I'm not regressing – or I'm trying not to. I made a promise to deliver this design by tomorrow. But I'll finish it in the morning. I will be leaving to come home in just a few minutes."

"See you whenever you get here – if I'm not asleep in bed by then," said Emily.

Bob did leave work a few minutes later and was soon home. Dinner was on the table and it was one of Bob's favorite meals, linguine with white clam sauce. But his mood did not equal the deliciousness of the pasta.

"You seem grumpy," Emily observed.

"Well, I don't appreciate it when you get snippy," Bob said. "I got deeply absorbed in solving some technical problems in this design I'm working on and I just wasn't paying attention to the time."

"You could have called."

"Yes, I could have! *If* I had known how late it was. Sorry. And I did not know you were making your incredibly wonderful linguine and your fabulous white clam sauce."

Emily smiled.

"Sucking up will get you ... anything you want," she said. "Would you like more linguine?"

"Yes, but no. I'm finally starting to lose some weight. I'm down nine pounds from the start of the month."

"That's great, Bob! And don't think I haven't noticed."

"Thank you."

"So tell me what got you so absorbed in whatever it is you're working on."

"It's not all that exciting," said Bob. "It's a design with a new approach to some difficult issues. Kind of boring actually."

"Boring? Then how come you were so involved you lost track of time?"

"Well, in fact, there *are* some interesting technical challenges – the kind I used to love to take on. But the main reason was that I promised Ned Meyers, the client, I would have the finished design by tomorrow. I've been putting him off for a month and it's now become a bit embarrassing. So in order to finish it, I had to block out everything else and focus."

"I don't mean to criticize, Bob. I'm just trying to understand. Why are you a month late?"

"There are a couple of reasons. One is the nature of the beast. Solving technical problems can't be done to a strict schedule because there are so many unknowables. As they say, you have the known unknowns and then you have the unknown unknowns – the things that pop up seemingly from nowhere and have to be dealt with."

"And the other reason?"

"It's a time trap. Custom design eats up the hours. And I have so many other matters to deal with – although a lot of progress has been made recently. From much improved cash management, to procedures that enable just about anyone to quickly learn any process, to bigger sales, to faster work flow, and so on – our situation is much better now. In fact, Emily, late in the afternoon I actually thought I would be able to come home early today. Then this thing with Ned cropped up."

"Can't someone else do these custom designs?" she asked.

"No, afraid not. I'm the only one in the company who can handle these because design work requires a lot of engineering expertise – as well as technical creativity, as well as the so-called people skills to build relationships with clients."

"What about hiring an engineer to handle it?"

"That's a thought. Trouble is, we don't really make all that much money from design projects. I'm not sure the sales for design projects would cover the engineer's salary."

"Then, Bob, why are you doing custom designs at all?"

"Because we as a company always have done them! In the early days of Burbells Universal, offering custom designs set us apart and gave us prestige. But not anymore, most customers are perfectly fine with standard designs. They cost less, they're readily available, and so on."

"This isn't adding up, Bob."

"I know. Actually, there are only a relative handful of customers who use the custom-design service. Ned is one, and I think we would lose all his business if we dropped the design capability."

"If you lost Ned's business, would that be a catastrophe?" Emily asked.

"No, not a catastrophe. Not financially. But Ned has been with us as a customer since the beginning. Maybe I'm being sentimental, but I would hate to lose him. He's part of our legacy."

"Legacies are rooted in the past, Bob. Don't you want products and customers that are oriented toward the future?"

Bob chuckled and said, "Yes, you're right."

Then his face took on an expression that was both thoughtful and astonished.

"What's the matter?" Emily asked.

"I might have to fire myself," he said with a wry smile. "One of our core values is that we aspire to simplicity. If we're offering both standard products and customized products, we're going the opposite way. We're increasing the complexity."

"Well, I don't know what to tell you about that."

"Maybe I'll ask Moe Strickett his opinion. I'm sure he'll have one. He always does."

*

The next day, Bob went to work quite early and finished the design. He then met with Ned later that morning to deliver it and discuss all the features and the nuances of each. With that load off his back, Bob got on the phone to Moe.

"What's up, Bob? Nothing too disastrous I hope."

"I'd like your perspective and insight on something – if you don't mind."

"Mind? Of course not. In fact, Bob, I'm rather flattered that you would turn to me."

"My intent is not to flatter you, but to gain advice on a segment of business strategy."

"You see, Bob, that is exactly what you should be doing as owner and leader – figuring out the best strategy to take the company to the next level. So what's the issue?"

"Burbells Universal has a design service. Only a few customers use it these days and I'm wondering if it makes sense to continue offering it. The service does make money overall, but its profitability is difficult to predict because of so many variables. And it consumes a lot of my own time, due to the fact that I am truly the only person in the company who can create the designs."

"You want my advice?" asked Moe.

"Yes."

"Dump it."

"But, Moe, let's not be entirely hasty!"

"Why not?"

"Because the design service is a part of who we are!"

"Listen, Bob, in the early days of Burbell technology, offering a design service perhaps made sense in order to bring in more customers by catering to their specialized needs. But now that the technology has matured and standard designs can accommodate the vast majority of needs, a design service just complicates matters and slows you down. It's not a profit builder. It's a distraction."

Bob sighed and said, "Yes, I suppose you're right. So what am I to do? Just shut it down? 'Dump it,' as you put it?"

"There are some choices," said Moe. "Indeed, you could just discontinue the service. You'll lose some customers, but you should be able to pick up others and operationally be more focused. Which makes everything a lot more efficient. Discontinuing it is the simplest thing to do, but you could also spin it off as a separate business if you can get the right personnel and make the numbers work. Or you might be able to sell the design service to someone else – although, since you personally are at the core of the service, it's questionable anyone would want it."

"I beg your pardon!"

"That's no reflection on you, Bob. I'm just stating reality."

"Moe, my main concern – and the reason I'm hesitating – is that our products are not one-size-fits-all, because our customers have different needs. The design service allowed for adaptability. And without it ... ? I mean, where are we headed? Are we just going to have one model, take or leave it?"

"You can still be adaptable. But do it with products, rather than through a service."

"Sorry, I don't understand."

"Options, Bob. Features and options. Instead of having a wide-open, infinitely variable, 'if you can imagine it we can build it' service, you instead create a limited range of specific models with different sets of features and options."

Inside Bob's mind, something connected and a light went on.

"Ah! I do understand what you're getting at! So we'd be enabling some flexibility for different needs – "

"But you would not have to reinvent the Burbell with each customized order," said Moe.

"Yes, now I get it!"

"Once you move in that direction, Bob, you're going to gain a lot of benefits. Your design happens once and then the product is sold in many thousands of copies. You'll eliminate the time pressure of having to come up with a fresh design for each customized order. Customers can pick and choose what suits their needs and you can quickly deliver what they've picked. It will be much easier to set sales targets because the margins will be known in advance. Marketing and advertising also become easier with tangible, established products rather than this vague, whatever-you-want design service. And so on."

"Yes, I'm seeing clearly what you're saying. And it's going to free me from having to do the design work. Which I used to love, but don't anymore. My only regret will be having to tell Ned and the others who used the service that it won't be available anymore."

"They'll get over it," said Moe.

*

Ned Meyers was indeed disappointed when Bob told him. Or at least he acted disappointed. The truth was that while he enjoyed coming up with new challenges for Bob, the designs also consumed a lot of his own time – and the expense of customization was not popular with his own corporate management. So Ned accepted the inevitable. Most importantly, Ned remained a customer and even increased his business with Burbells Universal because ordering was now much easier and faster than previously.

And thus Bob was able to eliminate another time trap from his work life, making life in general a lot better.

Chapter 23

The Dream

"Well, he did it again," Lena said.

"Who did what again?" Bob asked.

"Dennis. He installed the D-Packs backwards again. As a result we have dozens of units that are ruined."

"How could he do that?"

"Very easily," said Lena. "The D-Packs can be inserted either with the right side down *or* with the left side down. If it's left side down, the electronics are instantly fried as soon as the unit is switched on."

She shook her head.

"Poor Dennis ... " she said.

"What do you mean, 'poor' Dennis? Poor *me*! Poor customer! Poor company! Poor all of us!"

"What I meant is that Dennis tries hard to do the right thing. I'm not even sure the screw-up was really his fault."

"Not his fault? He made the mistake!"

"Yes, but what *allowed* him to make the mistake? Left side or right side, the D-Pack goes into its slot – with nothing to alert the assembler that it's going in the wrong way."

"What are you talking about?"

"The right side and the left side on the D-Pack look almost identical. On the right side there is a tiny white dot, but it can be easily overlooked. So unless you're paying very close attention one-hundred percent of the time, you can do it wrong. Right side or left, the D-Pack seats itself the same, with no indication that if it's done incorrectly the unit will be ruined."

"Show me," said Bob.

They went into Assembly and over to the workstation where the tragedy had occurred. Dennis was nearby looking quite sheepish. Lena demonstrated how easily the mistake could be made. Bob frowned.

"Are you going to fire me?" Dennis asked.

"No," said Bob, "because I can see now that the mistake you made was actually caused by a terrible design."

Dennis looked relieved.

"What I want you to do," Bob said to him, "is work with Lena and come up with a way to prevent this mistake from ever happening again."

"Right, Mr. Bingham."

"And Dennis, I think we know each other well enough by now. Just call me Bob."

"Thank you, Mr. Bingham. Er, Bob."

So Lena and Dennis got to work and within a short time had two solutions. One was a quick fix that could be implemented immediately: nail polish. Each D-Pack would be given a swipe of bright red nail polish on the right side – much more visible than a tiny white dot and nearly impossible to ignore.

The second solution was longer term to implement. They had to go to the D-Pack manufacturer and specify a redesigned shape that could only be inserted the correct way. But the redesign would take some time, so meanwhile they had good-old low-tech nail polish, which they had determined would not in any way affect the D-Pack's performance and would never be seen by customers.

*

Bob had lunch with Moe. They were getting along much better these days, though they still traded insults from time to time. Bob told Moe the story of the D-Pack problem.

"Poka-yoke," said Moe.

"Excuse me?"

"Poka-yoke is a Japanese word and concept referring to something becoming mistake-proof. Which is what you did with the D-Packs. Poka-yoke was developed by an industrial engineer named Shigeo Shingo. He also was involved in a number of other important concepts that were a part of the Toyota Production System."

"Ah, yes, TPS. I remember that from engineering school."

"Well, it's all still relevant," said Moe. "In fact, there is a well-established element of TPS known as kanban."

"Rings a distant bell," said Bob, "but what does 'kanban' do?"

"Kanban basically is an inventory management system of physical cards. The word more or less translates as a 'card you can see'. Written on the cards are refill orders for more components. When supply is running low, the kanban card is sent upstream to whatever will replenish the necessary supply. When the replenisher receives the card – or, these days, any medium that conveys the message – it creates the inventory and quickly sends it along so that it arrives 'just in time'. Which is a major component of TPS."

"Moe, I forget what I was taught so many years ago. What does kanban accomplish?"

"Kanban eliminates out-of-stocks that would cripple production while keeping inventories low. It's very important to think of work-in-process inventories as being not just so many pieces of whatever, but as being money. Inventory is money. It's money that has not as yet been turned into actual sales."

"And you think a kanban system would be good for Burbells Universal? I mean, we're not Toyota you know."

"True, you'll probably never be Toyota. But think a few steps ahead. Burbells Universal is growing. Whatever problems you have now are going to be enlarged in the future. So you need to install good systems now."

"Right," said Bob, "before the problems become gigantic."

"By the way," said Moe, "are you still looking forward to your trip to coconut land?"

"Oh, absolutely!" said Bob. "Very excited, every time I think of it."

"Good! I can just about see you in one of those grass skirts that they wear in the islands."

"Well, I'll bring you one of those, too, Moe. Then we can do the hula together."

*

The very next day, Bob became aware of a commotion going on in Assembly. He went to Lena.

"What's going on?" he asked.

"We've run out of thera-mods," she told him.

"Did you look – "

"We've looked everywhere. There are no thera-mods to be found. Bob, I'll take responsibility. I'll solve the problem. But we really do need to fix this. It seems as though we always have either too little or too much of everything."

"All right. Take care of the crisis, Lena. I'll stay out of your way, unless you need me. But once the crisis is behind us, we're going to put in place a kanban system."

"A what?"

"Kanban. Once you've rounded up the thera-mods, we'll talk about it."

And they did install a kanban system. Having done that, they never ran out of thera-mods – or anything else – ever again. Furthermore, they always had just the right amount, not too much and not too few.

*

One night shortly thereafter, Bob had a dream. Even as he was dreaming, he recognized that he had been in this dreamscape before.

He was in his office at work. Growing from the center of his desk was a tree – the greenest, tallest, most incredible tree Bob had ever seen. Fruit dangled from the branches of the tree – and not just low-hanging fruit. There was fruit ladening every branch bottom to top.

Bob felt himself being drawn to the tree. He was fascinated by it. And he began to climb it. Up and up and up. The climb – as it did occur in a dream – was effortless. He simply drifted upward, branch to branch.

Then Bob began to notice people in the tree. They were working, harvesting the fruit, doing things to help the fruit grow. Some were people he recognized – Felix, Alice, Kevin – while others were complete strangers, although Bob felt an affinity to them. He looked for Lena and finally spotted her, far up near the top. He waved to her and she waved back.

But he wanted to see the tree as a whole. He was in amongst the branches and holding onto the trunk, but he greatly wanted to see the total tree. Yet was afraid to. If he went out on a limb too far, he worried he might fall. Even so, he decided to take a chance. He stepped out onto a branch, farther and farther, and the tree still held him – until he stepped completely off. And he did not fall; he floated.

Now he could see the entire tree with all of its strengths and intricacies. He could see the people going about their work, everyone knowing what to do. He could see the beautiful fruit ripening before his eyes. And he felt very satisfied and happy.

Until the alarm clock went off. Bob silenced it while muttering a few choice grumpy words. The dream had vanished. Yet he knew it was still there. He knew the dream was real.

Chapter 24

The Future

Almost an entire year had passed. In that time, Burbells Universal had increased sales revenue by 50 percent and net income was up accordingly. Of course there still were issues, problems, and challenges; there always are. But the company was doing so well it was outgrowing the building.

"You're going to want to think about real estate," Moe said to Bob.

"I already am," said Bob.

"Are you? Very good! You know, you've come a long way."

"You can spare me the sarcasm."

"I wasn't being sarcastic, Bob. I was being sincere."

"You? Not being sarcastic?"

"Yes! You really have come a long way," said Moe. "Just look at what you're not doing!"

"*Not* doing?"

"Yes, what you're not doing. You're no longer meddling in the day-to-day operations. You're no longer micromanaging everything. You've stopped advancing the kind of customer credit that can ruin a business."

"True."

"On the other hand, look at what you *are* doing," said Moe. "You're hiring intelligently. You've got empowered teams now. You have an organization chart that is solid yet adaptable, offering a view of the future and what the company will grow into. You've put in place good systems. You've established easily understood core values that provide structure for decisions and behavior – and you really use them."

"Yes, I think all of those are worthwhile," said Bob.

"Not only that, but your standard procedures are such that practically anyone can read them and do the task. You have a scoreboard that shows real-time information about order status. And you did away with the custom design service, but instead focused on standard designs with various option packages."

"Right, and that's been working out well."

"Then there is K-Money, giving you a procedure that tells everybody whether the company is on track to meet its objectives every single day. You have KPIs that give you a heads-up on how well the company is executing. And you greatly improved operations by using a system constraint to regulate flow. Really, Bob, that's a lot to have accomplished in a year. You are to be commended. Well done!"

"I withdraw my own sarcasm," said Bob. "Thank you, Moe."

"However, there is one more thing I'd like to mention."

"What's that?"

"Coming at you rather soon, I think, will be one of the biggest challenges you'll ever face."

"And what might that challenge be?"

"The lack of challenges."

"Why would there be a lack of challenges?" Bob asked.

"Because of everything I just mentioned. The systems and procedures you put in place are largely running the business. That means you can stand back and let your staff do what you're paying them to do."

"So ... what am I supposed to do? Nothing?"

"Ah-ha! That is my point, Bob! It is so easy to stand back and do nothing. And if you allow that to happen ... ?"

"Life loses its meaning."

"Yes. Unfortunately, yes," said Moe. "It happened to me, you know. That was when I was still on 'business number one'. After a number of years of hard work, mistakes, and improvements – challenges – I had finally got everything sorted out. Everything fell into place. The business was running like a clock. And what happened to me? My life went flat. It lost its purpose. I became quite depressed. And I didn't know why."

"What did you do?" Bob asked.

"I had to fight my way out of it. I had to find ways to challenge *myself*. Which is what led me to open my second business. And later, my third and so on. There were personal quests as well. But those challenges I created for myself were what saved me from an empty life."

"Do you think that's going to happen to me?" Bob asked.

"Yes, I do. Not now, but eventually. Which is why I bring it up. You've got to be prepared so as not to fall into the trap of success. You've got to keep striving."

"Interesting," said Bob.

"Well, I usually am."

Chapter 25

Bob Stands Back

Nearly a year had passed and a number of things at Burbells Universal had changed – little things, as well as larger things. One of the little things was that Bob and Lena now alternated the task of picking up coffee and tea each morning from the deli across the street. For years, Lena alone had done this daily ritual because Bob had always come in so early that the deli was not even open yet. Now, they both came in at about the same time. So Bob would be on beverage duty one week and Lena would handle it the following week. In general, Bob had finally broken away from the workaholic regimen that had almost destroyed his life.

Among the larger changes, Burbells Universal was in fact growing into the organization chart created by Bob and Moe with input from Lena and a number of others. The company had leased space nearby for a second production facility to meet market demand. And they had been tuning processes to make them simpler. When they did this, they discovered that workflow improved.

When Bob delivered Lena's tea that morning, she had just started an operations meeting. It was a stand-up meeting with everybody in a circle. Standing tended to keep the meetings focused and short. Bob set Lena's tea on a table next to her.

"Thank you, Bob," she said.

"You know, I'd like to listen in if you don't mind," he said.

"Of course I don't mind," Lena said.

So Bob joined the circle and sipped his coffee while Lena's team went over the work orders. They talked about special concerns and needs and used the Scoreboard to establish priorities. Agreement was quickly reached.

"Are there any other issues that need to be discussed?" Lena asked.

For a moment, everyone was quiet. Then Kevin signaled that there was something he wanted to talk about.

"I think the NanoWelder might be about to fail. It's been cutting out lately for no reason and that's usually a bad sign. I don't know when, but it might totally quit on us."

Bob's brain instantly went into hyper-drive. He had personally dealt with this same situation several times over the years. And he knew all the answers.

"We can get it repaired, can't we?" asked Felix.

No! No, you want it rebuilt, not repaired, thought Bob. *And the best way to go is to look for a used one!*

Bob wanted desperately to provide the answer. He started to open his mouth, but an inner voice told him, *Don't spoil it for them. Let them figure it out on their own.*

"Actually, I think it would be better to have it rebuilt," said Kevin. "The trouble is that for it to be rebuilt we'll have to part with it for a fairly long time."

Yes! For a rebuild, you're talking two to four weeks, thought Bob. *And where is its replacement in the meantime?*

But he was able to hold his tongue by biting on it.

"Well, the problem," said Lena, "is where is its replacement in the meantime? What do we do for a NanoWelder while ours is being rebuilt?"

"Can't we just buy a new one?" asked Felix.

"We could, but they're very expensive," said Kevin.

"Yes, we should explore cheaper alternatives first," said Lena.

Find a used one! Bob wanted to shout.

"Could we rent one while ours is being rebuilt?" asked Kevin.

A rental? Bob thought as he continued to bite his tongue. *Yes, that's worth consideration.*

"You know, I think that's a possibility," said Lena. "Kevin, can you take that on? Check with the equipment rental outfits and see if we can rent a NanoWelder?"

"Sure, I can do that," said Kevin.

"Good. And let me know right away if our NanoWelder gets worse."

Bob allowed his teeth to release his tongue. He was still tempted to mention his own idea of searching for a used NanoWelder, but he kept quiet.

Instead, Bob stepped back. He stood outside the circle while the others continued to talk.

"Excuse me, Bob, but are you leaving?" Lena asked.

"Yes, you and your team have all this well in hand," Bob said. "So I am going to go contemplate some blue-sky possibilities for the company's next venture. Carry on!"

He then went to his office, enjoyed his coffee, and doodled – in the hope that his little sketches might inspire innovation now or over time.

Lena came in a short while later.

"You were dying to jump in and solve all our problems, weren't you," she said to Bob.

He smiled.

"Yes. I was."

"Thank you for not doing that," Lena said.

"You're welcome."

*

Bob checked his calendar and saw that his two-week vacation was fast approaching. He had booked the trip the year before at Moe Strickett's urging. He had let Emily make the final choice of the destination. Yet, at that time, Bob had questioned whether it would even be possible for him to be away for such an incredibly long period of time. Two weeks?! How many things could go wrong over the course of two weeks! Why, the possibilities seemed infinite! And he would not be on the scene to fix whatever went wrong.

But as the months went by and the new systems and procedures were put into place, Bob began to have confidence that maybe he actually could be away for an extended period. Over the weeks and months, the confidence and competence of everyone in the company, not just Bob's, had risen. Guided by the core values and empowered to create their own solutions, the employees and the team leaders now fixed most everyday problems on their own, with no need for intervention by Bob.

That is not to say that Bob had nothing to do all day. On the contrary, he had plenty to do. He still maintained relationships with the top managers of their largest customers. He was vigilant over finances and knew where the company stood with respect to cash, expenses, receivables, and so on. He was forever looking for and exploring ways to improve company performance. Etc., etc. But the number of day-to-day issues were now greatly reduced and easily handled by Lena and others before they escalated to crisis status. This tremendously lightened Bob's load.

So why not get away and have some fun?

*

With his departure date looming, Bob threw himself into finishing everything that he had to finish. He was perhaps the most efficient he had ever been, knowing that the trip was in effect a deadline and there were only so many hours available until then. But it was exciting as well in the way that mad dashes often can be.

On the last day, Bob worked until five o'clock, then went to Lena with a short list of things she should be aware of in his absence.

"And that's it!" Bob declared. "I am out of here! And Lena, I only want to hear from you in the event of an extreme emergency. Like the world ending."

"Have a good time, Bob. You deserve it," she told him.

When Bob got home, his wife greeted him with a warm hug and a kiss, and Bob returned the favor.

"Emily, I am a free man!" he announced.

"Good," she said, "keep it that way."

Early the next morning, they were seated next to each other on the plane as it was being readied for takeoff. Bob sat back and thought about the day when Moe had driven the two of them to the airport where they had watched a Sunn Airlines jet aircraft take off into the wild blue – with no direct assistance of the airline's founder and CEO, James Sunn. Now here he was, seated in a Sunn aircraft, ready to enjoy two weeks in a faraway place and with no connection to – and no serious worries about – the company. Bob could hardly have imagined such a thing just a year before. Back then, to leave the business for any extended period of time? Unthinkable!

"What are you grinning about?" Emily asked.

"Everything," he said.

A number of hours later, they were flying over a tropical paradise. The plane safely landed – still without direct assistance from the airline's CEO. A driver in a golf cart took them to the resort. They checked in. They went to their suite, where Bob stepped onto the balcony and watched the surf pounding on the sandy beach. And the first thing Bob did after that?

Absolutely nothing.

*

For the entire two weeks, Bob's phone did not ring. Indeed, aside from a few calls to family and friends, Bob hardly touched his phone. And, as the world did not end, Lena did not call.

Toward the end of their stay, Emily told Bob that in all their years together, she had never seen him so relaxed and at peace with himself. And that harmonious state of mind did not entirely evaporate once Bob returned to Burbells Universal. He was able to stay in that zone, as they say, and the more he did this, the longer the sensibilities lasted.

This is not to say that all was perfect. The situation Bob encountered when he got back was pretty good, but there had been some slip-ups. Lena and Bob talked and concluded that there were some systemic weaknesses – but also that the systems could be strengthened.

Then Bob met with Moe and handed him a coconut.

"Thank you, but where is my grass skirt?" Moe asked.

"Oh, damn. Forgot it."

"That's perfectly all right, Bob. Not a problem! Now tell me, how's the company doing?"

Bob gave him a rundown, mentioning the weaknesses.

"Yes," said Moe, "there will be weaknesses and they especially reveal themselves in a small business when the owner is away. Because even though you have transferred most operational responsibilities to those better able to manage them, you are still a presence and a stopgap. So while you were away, the weaknesses presented themselves. Which actually is an opportunity."

"What do you mean?" asked Bob.

"Well, it's been said that every problem is an opportunity in disguise," said Moe. "I tend to agree with that – and even look forward to it, since most managers on the other side of the competitive fence will try to cover up the problems, even say they don't exist."

They were walking toward the airport, toward their bench. The sky was cloudy. No rain though, not as yet.

"Believe me, Bob, human nature doesn't change by much. While they are covering up, if you can recognize and diagnose the problem and then take action, you're going to be on the winning end. Seriously, it's an opportunity."

"All right," said Bob, "but speaking of opportunities, why not a whole new business? I mean, I had an idea ... "

"You, Bob? An idea? Really?"

"Yes, Moe, you prick. An idea. It's just a little idea right now. But in time, it might well be bigger in impact than Burbells by an order of magnitude."

They came to their bench overlooking the airport runway. They sat down.

"All right, tell me about it," said Moe.

"Please? I mean, shouldn't you add that?"

"Fine. Will you *please* tell me about it."

And they talked for hours at their bench near the airport. They are working on the concept even now.

# # #

Next steps

1. Review

If you have enjoyed Stand Back To Grow, we will be honored to have it positively reviewed on Amazon. This will help promote the book, which in turn will help in reaching out to other overwhelmed business owners who desperately need it.

2. Recommend

If you know someone who will benefit from Stand Back To Grow, please recommend it to them too!

3. Visit

Visit www.standbacktogrow.com to begin your Stand Back To Grow journey today. Whether you are seeking direct support, further education, or looking to join a community of like-minded individuals who share your passion for business, this website is your gateway to a wealth of information and engagement.

4. Live a meaningful life!

There is more to life than just running a business, so act now and get your life back!

www.standbacktogrow.com